Hertfordshire

D1440044

520 610 81 X

Many of the columns you'll find in this book have appeared on
www.rubbishlesbian.com
and in DIVA magazine either in print or online at
www.divamag.co.uk

Follow me @rubbishles and DIVA @DIVAmagazine on Twitter

December 2013


ISBN Number: 978-0-9928996-0-8



Cover shot by Lucy Pope
www.lucypope.com

Styling by Kate Wingrove, Trevor Sorbie, London

Book design by SWATT Design Ltd
www.swatt-design.co.uk

Published by Mimwood Press

MIMWOOD
PRESS

Printed and bound by CPI Group (UK) Ltd
Croydon, CR0 4YY

**To the rubbish lesbian in all of us.**

# Contents

**FOREWORD** **1**

**INTRODUCTION** **3**

**PART ONE: LESBIAN SEX** **5**

Lesbian Sex. What's Hard About That? 6

Let's Talk About Sex, Straight Friend. 8

Fat Fingering is Not a Lesbian Sex Act. 10

Different Strokes: "What'chu talkin' bout Clitoris?" 12

Lesbian Threesomes: Three Times the Fun, or a Three-ring Circus? 14

A Sex-Toy Story (To Infinity and Beyond!). 16

I Don't Dream of Angie: Why Can't I Have a Lesbian Sex Dream? 18

Confessions of a Cock Encounter. 20

Meatballs to Your Straight Innuendo. 22

The Sausage Botherers: Dick Jokes That'll Make You Gag. 24

**PART TWO: COMING OUT** **27**

Coming Out: What Took Me So Long? 28

Every Day is Coming Out Day. 30

Checking In, Coming Out: Is There No Escaping the Awkwardness? 32

A Blast from My Heterosexual Past. 34

Coming Out Lessons From My Father. 36

Actually, I'm a Lesbian: How to Correct Assumptions About Your Sexuality. 38

Is it Ever Okay to Go Back in the Closet? 40

**PART THREE: FAMILY AND FRIENDS** 43

How to Perform a Lesbocism: Straightening up the House. 44

Mum's the Word: Hot Lesbian Couple Hits Port Douglas. 46

It's Christmas (But Don Me Not My Gay Apparel). 48

Cats, Kids and Turkey Basters. 50

Big Brogues to Fill: Assuming the Role of Pseudo Son-in-Law. 52

The Breasts of Friends: Are Some Boobs Not Up For Grabs? 54

Talking Man-To-Man: I Talk Business With the Boys. 57

The Time I Accidentally Described My Girlfriend as Slutty. To Her Parents. 59

No Sex Please, You're Lesbians: the In-Laws' Open Door Policy. 61

It's Christmas and We're Keeping Feelings Under Wraps. 63

**PART FOUR: RELATIONSHIPS** 65

Public Displays of Distraction: Unsure About PDA. 66

"No, we're not sisters": Dealing With Sibling Assumptions. 68

Too Many 'Babes': Finding the Perfect Pet Name. 70

"When are we getting our period?" 72

Out of Sync: A Miserable Menstrual Relay. 74

Lesbian Bath Death. The Beginning of the End? 76

Snuggle Politics: The Flipside of Snuggling. 78

The Wrong Trousers: Dealing with Clothing Mix-Ups. 80

The Mane is the Bane of the Long-haired Lesbian Couple. 82

Feline Interruptus: It's Sex or the Cat. 85

**PART FIVE: OUT AT WORK** 87

The Conversational Cul-de-Sac: Playing the Pronoun Game. 88

Alter Ego Trip, or Why it's Not a Good Idea to Invent a Boyfriend. 90

Does my Bum look Gay in This? Wearing a Skirt to the Office. 92
Everybody Out: Accidentally Coming Out to the New Girl During a Fire Alarm. 94
Being in the Closet at the Office is Too Much Like Hard Work. 96
One Small Room at the Holiday Inn: Sharing a Bed with a Colleague. 98
The Office Christmas Party: Suddenly Everyone's a Lesbian. 101

**PART SIX: LESBIAN STEREOTYPES** **103**

Lesbian Relationships: The Unwritten Roles. 104
Rocking the Bandana, or I Get My Butch On. 106
I'm Officially a Red-Lipstick Lesbian. 108
IKEA – A Little Trip Into Bank Holiday Hell Anyone? 110
I'm Very Sporty: I Love to Watch. 112
Crazy Cat Ladies Host a Lip Service Dinner Party. 114
Directionally Challenged: If in Doubt, Keep Going Straight. 116

**PART SEVEN: SHIT PEOPLE SAY** **119**

"You're a lesbian. Great! We're totally fine with that." 120
"I wish I was a lesbian." 122
"What a waste!" 124
"You've gone a bit too gay." 126
"But dude, who's the groom?" 128
"It's a wonderful lesbian lifestyle." 130
"I'd make a good lesbian." 132
"I know another lesbian, not very well." 134
"But you're not one of those lesbians!" 137

**PART EIGHT: LESBIAN FAILS** **139**

Not Stalking But (Flat) Hunting. 140

An Inappropriate Kiss: A Warm Welcome Gets Out Of Hand. 142

Nail Fail: The Art Of Coming Out Over a Manicure. 144

My Birthday Massage Has a Happy Ending. 146

Seeing Eye-To-Eye With My Optician. 148

A Soapy Revelation at the Vet. 150

Out Of My Depth: Awkward Times in the Swimming Pool Changing Room. 152

Out, Very Loud and Not So Proud in Currys. 154

The Salesman Of My Dreams: Going Mattress Shopping With My Girlfriend. 156

Pride Dashed: When a Wedding Clashes With a Gay Celebration. 158

Dropping a Table, and the L-Bomb. 160

Bikini-Clad Awkwardness Anyone? Outed by the Holiday Rep. 162

The Sun's Popped Out, and I'm Busted. 164

This is Not My Corsa: Bumping Into An Old Flame. 166

**PART NINE: OTHER LESBIANS** **169**

I Need a Gaydar Upgrade. 170

Sadly, Not Gay Enough for One Girl. 172

The Lesbian Effect: It Makes Women More Interesting. 174

Lesbian Bars Are Not My Scene. 176

Flirting With Disaster: Caught With Ink On My Face. 178

How to Survive a Celesbian-Packed Party. 180

The Lesbian Nod: It's Like The Bus-Driver's Wave. 182

The Lesbian Network: Six Inches of Separation. 184

Honest, I'm a Lesbian: A Case of Mistaken Sexual Identity. 186

**AFTERWORD** **188**

# FOREWORD

Long before I ever met Sarah Westwood I was a fan of her Rubbish Lesbian column. For the last three years she has entertained us with the idiosyncrasies, insecurities and joys of navigating a lesbian lifestyle. Whether it's coming out, staying in, bra shopping with a straight friend or accidentally implying your girlfriend is 'slutty' to her parents, she has left no lesbian stone unturned. One thing the Rubbish Lesbian definitely isn't rubbish at is writing. There are enough laugh out loud anecdotes, witty one liners and heartfelt observations here to make David Sedaris look over his shoulder anxiously. So when she asked me to introduce this collection, I jumped at the chance. Partly because if someone's writing appeals to me I like to bang on about it. Also because, given the opportunity to avoid my own writing, I grasp it with both hands. There is, after all, only so many times you can tidy your filing cabinet or watch that video on YouTube that tells you how to fold up your T shirts so they look like they're on a shop shelf.

Sarah was initially inspired to write this column so she could gently poke fun at her coming-out anxieties. Anyone who has ever been through the experience will find something to empathise with here. With laser-like precision and wit she presents a smorgasbord of the potential awkwardnesses of the experience. Reading about her concerns over visiting a gay club transported me back to my own early worries around going to a gay venue. How I tackled this dilemma by trying to find a girlfriend in my local library. After many hours spent hanging around the lesbian and gay aisle waiting for a girlfriend to materialise, I realised it was never going to work. So I upped my game and got a job in a gay bookshop. That way I'd definitely get to talk to real lesbians, even if it was only to ask them whether they'd like a bag with that.

Over the years, Sarah's column has expanded into new territory, exploring the myriad of ways she feels like a rubbish lesbian and the ways other people are rubbish around lesbians. When I recently met Sarah for the first time I was struck by how someone who has been so eloquent about her anxieties appeared so calm and collected. It made me realise what's so brilliant about this column. In laying bare her insecurities for all to read, she has exposed the veneer of confidence we adopt to cover up our 'rubbishness.' Next time you ask yourself the question, is it just me?, you will know the answer is no, it's Sarah and probably most other people too.

I was reminded of our capacity to veer from confidence to anxiety in a nanosecond when Sarah and I had lunch recently. It's a fact that ninety percent of women who love women love cats. OK, that's a lie, I made it up, but it sounds about right so let's just go with it. We were chatting about our feline friends when she casually mentioned her cat's hot water bottle. Hang on, I thought, rewind, her hot water bottle! Having been enjoying my baba ganoush, I was besieged by rubbish lesbian style panic. I've never given my cat a hot water bottle. I thought he was as spoilt as a cat could be. But had I been so busy plying him with organic cat treats, scratching his chin and taking pictures of him dressed as a matador that I'd failed to see he was deprived of warmth? Am I, well frankly, a bit rubbish?

~ Harriet Braun

# INTRODUCTION

The Rubbish Lesbian began as a form of therapy. I was struggling with my identity as a lesbian, and I wasn't really open to the idea of actual therapy. I tried it: for one hour a week I'd sit and stare silently back at the sympathetic-looking woman in a patchwork coat, and think, "This isn't for you. Spend the fifty pounds on M&S underwear". When my therapist suggested I try moulding my feelings out of plasticine, I left therapy, bought some new pants, and started writing for DIVA magazine.

The thing was, though I'd come out to family and friends at 30 I didn't take to being a lesbian like a duck to water, unless the duck in question was a horrible swimmer with a terrible case of internalised aquaphobia. The year I came out, Bush was hell-bent on trying to get into the White House. I'd like to say that I quipped that I was hell-bent on getting bush, but those words would never have passed my lips.

The Rubbish Lesbian was a way to poke fun at my own discomfort, to be honest with myself and others about my own insecurities. I had an idea that being a good lesbian meant always being confident about it, out and proud, and I felt that I fell short. Lesbians mistook me for straight, and straight friends thought I was a rubbish lesbian, because I had long hair and thought WD40 was the robot from Star Wars.

I was rubbish at meeting women, and the idea of the 'lesbian scene' terrified me. I imagined it involved attending a series of queer subterranean club nights with names like Twat and Snatch, where hungry lesbians would launch themselves at me like I was the last sausage roll at a wedding buffet. It seemed completely at odds with my idea of a good night, which involved beans on toast and an Attenborough documentary.

I wasn't prepared for the fact I'd have to come out to people who assumed I was straight on an almost daily basis. I felt I was hiding something, like a kid who'd broken a vase and didn't know how or when to 'come clean'. I rarely owned the situation quickly enough, so I'd either leave it too late and blurt "he's a woman!" having allowed them to talk about my boyfriend for the last hour, or helplessly keep schtum and silently hate myself.

The Art of the Casual Come Out during chats with the vet or that flirty bloke at the dry cleaners baffled me with the limitless ways it could go pear-shaped. Assuming I was straight, my greengrocer had for years greeted my purchases with his stock phrase, "your fella's getting looked after well." When I set him straight, his trademark greeting seemed to my self-conscious ears to have a different ring to it. As I reached for a decent sized banana and he said, "She's getting well looked after", I was so embarrassed I never went back, which is a shame because he had the straightest courgettes in town.

I've written over 60 columns to date about life as a 'Rubbish Lesbian', covering everything from the horror of correcting a hotel receptionist who's moved us to a double room where we'll be "much more comfortable" to my often slippery grasp of boob etiquette. I've shared my experience of being treated like 'the man' in the relationship by my girlfriend's parents, to navigating the social minefield of not being out at work, like the time I backed myself into a conversational corner with a colleague and, running out of pronouns, almost described my girlfriend as 'it'.

When, on occasion, people have tweeted me to tell me that a column has struck a chord, I think it's because as a lesbian no matter how long you've been out, or how many people you're out to, there's always a new real estate agent with assumptions to correct, or an awkward social moment to deal with. And if we're honest there's probably a rubbish lesbian in all of us.

PART ONE

# LESBIAN SEX

## First Times, Sex Toys and a Cock Encounter.

*Many people hear the word lesbian and think 'sex'. So I'm just going to accept that that's what people are interested in, and get down to sex first. For me having sex with a woman for the first time wasn't a walk in the park. It was more of a lung-busting trek to Machu Picchu in a hailstorm, after 13 shots of tequila.*

*I've written about everything from actually 'doing it', to my inability to talk sex with my straight friends, and my subconscious, dogged refusal to stop dishing up nightly heterosexual sex dreams. I've even thrown in some sex toys, a sausage or two, and a cock mention. So hopefully there's a little something for everyone.*

*Be under no illusion, the following anecdotes will shed no light whatsoever on the mystery that is Lesbian Sex; we can only hope that by applying themselves night and day to the task Jessica Fletcher and Miss Marple will crack that one day soon.*

*You'd think a woman having sex with another woman would be easy because you are much more familiar with the equipment. Okay, so it's not as tough as the Telegraph crossword, but I found it surprisingly difficult.*

## Lesbian Sex. What's Hard About That?

I thought having sex with a woman would be easy – after all, I'm far more intimate with all the equipment involved. It's also quite liberating not to be operating under the ever-present threat of a penile explosion that could take an eye out at any minute. And yet for some reason I found sex with a woman much harder than with a man.

In my experience, pulling off good sex with a man was relatively easy: show up and you're 90% there; show up dressed as a sexy nurse and you can take that up to 98%. But women are much harder to please. I know this for a fact, because I am one.

Lesbian sex looks easy enough in the movies. Take Bound: one minute you're idly eyeing up your hot new neighbour, the next thing you know Gina Gershon has popped around to fix a leaky tap and you're having mind-blowing sex. But in reality there's a little more to it.

The thing is, we've all been on the receiving end of someone going down on us like an I'm a Celebrity contestant face down in a box of cockroaches fishing for stars with their mouth. Nobody wants to be that person. All women are different; there are millions of nuances, which means there are millions of ways I could get it wrong.

Add to that the fact that it's complete and utter anarchy. No one is in charge and yet everyone is in charge, because roles are thrown out the window with gay abandon. There is no obvious timeframe – with no penis driving the timings this thing could go on all night.

Then comes the real head fuck. The big question I never really worried about with a man. What are they thinking? I bet they're thinking my M&S pants need retiring, or I thought her boobs would be bigger. There's so much thinking going on we could levitate out of there. Not so much sex as a display of Jedi mind tricks.

Meanwhile my brain is flooding with emotions. I'm happy, really I am, so why do I feel like I might burst into tears when we get to the good bit, like an overwhelmed toddler at their own birthday party. I feel really exposed. There is no place to hide. There's no pretence or artifice, because women are in on the secret. This is the hardest thing about lesbian sex. Intimacy.

Then it happens. Against all odds I've managed to pull it off. Holy crap, I feel invincible. I must have a bit of a talent; it wasn't that hard after all.

And suddenly it's as if I've been let in on a really big secret God, no wonder men are so full of themselves. Who wouldn't be?

*My straight friends have been amazingly supportive and in fact many of them had enjoyed 'brushes with lesbianism' way before I made it popular. I wrote the following column early on in 2011, because although I'd happily discuss male conquests with ease I found I was far more reticent when it came to talking about women. I think I worried about grossing them out or making them feel uncomfortable, which I later realised had far more to do with my own internalised homophobia.*

## Let's Talk About Sex, Straight Friend.

Some things are best left unsaid, particularly over a coffee and pancakes with your straight friends. "You should never have married him". "You have an ugly baby". Or, if you are a rubbish lesbian like me, "Last night my girlfriend and I were doing it and…."

Before I became the rubbish lesbian I am today, I was a very proficient straight girl. I had regular girlie brunches with my other straight friends and the topic of sex often came up. No subject was deemed too personal or private. No conversational crevice left unprobed. Girls just love to talk about sex.

Then I became a lesbian and the sex chat dried up quicker than (insert own sexual innuendo). It's as if I have been literally struck dumb. Clammed up. When the subject of sex comes up, I slink back in my chair hoping no one will pick me. I have no problem doing 'it', so why do I dry up when it comes to talking about sex with girls?

Firstly, I'm embarrassed. It feels different now – both the sex and the talk. Also, I don't feel equipped. I have an impotent struggle for the right words but nothing comes. I'm worried I might sound like a straight porn star. 'Pussy' just doesn't come naturally. Worse still, I might sound like a man. If I say, "She's got great tits!" they'll accuse me of objectifying women (which of course I would be). I worry about using words they've never heard before. Words that might give away my difference – the fact I am a lesbian. They might start viewing me differently –no longer one of the girls.

Inevitably, on a drunken night someone will corner me for 'the truth.' Come on, what's it really like to have sex with a woman? Still I give them a muted version. Not forthright, not shocking -- not convincing.

Why? Am I trying to spare their embarrassment or mine?

Maybe the truth is I don't want to open Pandora's Box. Part of the joy of talking about having 'straight' sex is how hit and miss it can be. There's great camaraderie in the battle tales, a whole lexicon dedicated to disappointment. That's something we can all get behind, laugh about and bond over. So imagine the reaction to my true tales of what happened last night: not laughing, not bonding, just stunned silence.

The truth? They can't handle the truth. The sex was really good.

*God if I had a pound for the number of times the question of what is lesbian sex, or is it even really sex, came up I'd be rich and living in Maui having every kind of lesbian sex you can imagine – or not imagine – as the case may be.*

## Fat Fingering is Not a Lesbian Sex Act.

I mentioned my habit of 'fat-fingering' to a straight friend this week. She went very quiet, and then said, "Is that a lesbian thing?" What? No, it's an inability to use an iPhone thing. It made me laugh, but it also made me realise that lesbian sex is still the big question mark that remains unanswered for a lot of people. In the words of 80s songstress Toyah, "it's a mystery."

I've been asked, "But how DO you have sex?" on many occasions. It seems odd, but for whatever reason many people just can't get their heads around lesbian sex. Maybe I'm just particularly flexible, but I've never found it that much of a strain.

Even before I became a lesbian, if I closed my eyes I could picture it with ease, and did, on many occasions. The image wasn't sketchy, and it didn't fade-to-black like a 1940s film when it got to the good bit. But for many people lesbian sex remains as baffling as the Bermuda Triangle – actually make that two Bermuda Triangles rubbing together.

In the past when I've talked about 'having sex', to some of my straight girlfriends I've noticed that their faces fail to compute. They have the look of someone reading the assembly instructions for an IKEA bedside table. It's as if they are sitting cross-legged on the floor with all of our bits laid out in front of them, and they just can't picture how we'll come together.

I think it's the lack of penis that throws people; their minds are desperately grappling with the logistics of how sex is possible without one. It's hard to know what goes where; like a game of naked Twister, there are body parts swinging around, and skin slapping against skin, but they can't see the wood for the trees. Perhaps because there is no wood, or trees – only bushes?

What is it about two women having sex that's so hard to imagine? It's not as if we're aliens from planet Zorb with paint brushes for genitals. We've got all the same bits as straight women, and like them sex comes down to personal preference. There's no one-size-fits-all answer.

We might have put people on the moon, but for some reason lesbian sex is one giant mental leap too far. Oh well, as long as it remains the final frontier I'll just have to keep on boldly going where no man has gone before.

*From memory, the first time I slept with a woman my technique was to randomly push buttons, the same tactic I use when I play PlayStation with my nephew. Thankfully we both emerged relatively unscathed; her with some mild bruising, and me with a new empathy for the men I'd dated.*

## Different Strokes: "What'chu talkin' bout Clitoris?"

Chances are that like me, at some point you'll have experienced someone going down on you with the technique of a drunken apple bobber at a Halloween party. I never understood why some men found cunnilingus so perplexing. It seemed like a no-brainer. In my head I'd be tutting impatiently, like someone anxiously waiting in line at the supermarket self-checkout unable to fathom why the bloke in front is repeatedly scanning a persimmon with no bar code sticker on it. It's not until I had to step up myself that I realised how sensitive the machine is to an unexpected item in the bagging area.

I'm not going to beat around the bush, pleasuring a woman is a tough nut to crack. Actually it's more like safe cracking. It's a matter of having the right tools, the right skills and plenty of patience. Even if you know the combination (and the combination changes), it's still possible to buckle under the pressure, beads of sweat tracing their way down your forehead as you consider the humiliation if you can't crack it and have to emerge casually from the duvet pretending you've been in the other room reading a book all this time. "Tea love?"

It doesn't help matters that you're often completely sensorily deprived and pinned down by the weight both of expectation and a 14 tog John Lewis duvet. Any feedback is muffled and impossible to decipher because you're wearing a very tight fitting pair of thigh earmuffs. Nor can you see what's going on. There should be an inbuilt automatic light that comes on, like the one in a car bonnet, to allow you to look under the hood. If you're still flying blind in the final moments it's often better to disengage the navigation system, close your eyes, and trust in the force, like a young Luke Skywalker with only one shot left to hit the tiny target that will destroy the Death Star.

Even as a woman it can be hard to understand what another woman wants and read the signals. As the saying goes, it's different strokes for different folks. "What'chu talkin' bout clitoris?" Dealing with the clitoris can be like dealing with a colleague suffering from PMT. Sometimes they're impatient and it's best just to get in quick and be direct. Other times they're extra sensitive and you have to take a softly, softly approach. Then they just go off at you for seemingly no reason leaving you open mouthed and stunned. If you're friendly and they don't respond it's best to just give them a wide berth.

*This column came about after a discussion I had with a friend about threesomes. It was not, I hasten to add, the kind of discussion that ends, "...wouldn't it be fun, do you fancy it?"*

## Lesbian Threesomes: Three Times the Fun, or a Three-ring Circus?

It's a truth universally acknowledged that a straight man of a certain age is always up for a threesome with a couple of buxom 'lesbians', preferably the kind who won't mind if he slips in a small suggestion of his own. The lesbians I know wouldn't touch that with a barge pole. But what if it were another woman?

I don't really see the appeal of lesbian threesomes. Any more than one bird at a time seems a little greedy: the sexual equivalent of a Turducken. Sure, a turkey stuffed with duck stuffed with a chicken might sound like a fun and experimental meal, but in the end if you really love duck you only want duck, and the turkey's just an elaborate distraction.

The whole thing just sounds like an awful lot of hard work. There's too much going on at once. Yes, you've got an extra pair of hands, but you've also got an extra pair of tits to worry about. Juggling two extra boobs wouldn't leave a lot of time for anything else. One lady would be going off the boil, and you'd have to go back and get her going again, tweaking away like a sort of demented plate spinner.

Were I to find myself entangled in a ménage a trois I'd worry about getting left out, and feeling like a third wheel. It would be like visiting Blackpool pleasure beach with two more adventurous friends; the sorts that would run off and leave me holding the coats and Cokes. They might be riding high on The Big One, but I'd be the one getting shafted.

And what happens afterwards? I suspect it's like taking that ill-advised third trip up to the all-you-can-eat buffet: It might seem a good idea when you're all worked up and in the moment, but it heralds an onslaught of gut-wrenching remorse that no amount of Rennie can assuage. Cue a night spent on the toilet head-in-hands asking yourself whatever possessed you to go for another helping.

With so many reservations, I fear that the only time I'm likely to see three bras on the floor is the first day of the M&S sale. I know we're told that good things come in threes, but I think lesbians should always come in twos.

*In this column I grasp the slippery subject of sex toys. In the early days what I knew about lesbian sex I gleaned from the tabloids, where 'lesbian romps' always seemed to involve lots of giggling and a dildo the size of an Easter Island statue. I think that's many people's perception of what constitutes lesbian sex.*

## A Sex-Toy Story (To Infinity and Beyond!).

How do you introduce a new sex toy without making your partner feel inadequate, as if, like Woody, they're not measuring up, and you're looking to add a little Buzz? Probably best not to just whip it out from under the pillow and brandish it aloft yelling "To infinity and beyond!". Better to try to involve them in the decision way before it gets to this point.

Be aware that the dildo conversation can blow Pandora's Box wide open. You need to approach the subject with care, from the right angle. Don't plunge head first into the topic, but work it in gently, preferably after lubricating them thoroughly with a nice glass of Sangiovese.

If you're both into it, it can be a lot of fun to go shopping together. If at any point you get embarrassed and don't want the shop assistants to know you're a lesbian couple, here's my top tip: when you've made your selection pick up some penis straws and they'll assume that you're two chums. They'll think the whole thing is a lark and that you're not really going to rush home and jab each other silly. No, you're just shopping for a hen night. What larks!

If you're too embarrassed to browse, buy the first thing you see that's light enough to carry and get the hell out of there. I call this the 'smash and grab' technique. But bear in mind it's a bit hit and miss, and you may well get home with nothing more to show for your efforts than a bejewelled butt plug. Speaking of regretted purchases I can also say from personal experience it's best not to go pissed. I once visited a sex shop in the West Village in New York at 4am after a dozen margaritas and it turned out my eyes were bigger than my fanny (a tiny point of clarification, I'm using fanny in the English sense of the word).

When you get them home it's customary to give your new toy a cute nickname. Nothing ruins an intimate moment quite like having to pop your head up from under the duvet to ask politely "could you pass me the Mains Powered Deluxe Water Proof Magic Wand in pink when you get a moment please?" Far better to say "Is your lil friend there?". Sex toys are not the enemy; they are a powerful re-chargeable ally in the fight for good. You've got a friend in me, indeed.

*This column is my favourite, because I sat down and wrote it in one go after waking up from the dream detailed. I found it really intriguing that just at the point I was starting to accept myself as a lesbian, my subconscious was still holding fast to the idea of me being straight, and that this manifested itself in an inability to dream about lesbian sex.*

## I Don't Dream of Angie: Why Can't I Have a Lesbian Sex Dream?

People say that dreaming in a different language is a good indicator of fluency in that language. Well, I'm clearly not yet fluent in lesbian, because I still have heterosexual sex dreams.

Obviously there's some dark corner of my psyche that refuses to accept the fact that I'm gay. It lurks somewhere deep in the recesses of my brain, where a crush on Gary Barlow makes its last stand to the soundtrack from Top Gun.

My self-conscious must be really lesbophobic, because in the past I've even had a sex dreams involving a male pilot. I'm terrified of flying, so a cock within a cockpit is the Russian doll of disturbing sex dreams for me.

Even on the odd occasion that I managed to sneak a woman past my sleeping subconscious the joy was short lived. We'd be getting it on and I'd look down to find I was getting it up. My twisted mind had made me the man of my dreams. You know what they say, if you can't spot the dick in the room it's probably you – that turned out to be true in my case.

It's very frustrating. Even my straight girlfriends have had lesbian sex dreams, but for some reason I've never got lucky.

But wait, a breakthrough; I'm suddenly having a dream involving Angelina Jolie. At last! She had just moved in next door and popped round, in a white tank top, to borrow a cup of sugar! I know, a likely story, but I'll go along with it for now.

All I want is to put my failure to dream in lesbian to bed – preferably with Angelina – but I'm distracted. My brain is saying, "If she's moved in next door what's happened to our neighbour?" "Forget John", another part of my brain is shouting, "It's a dream remember? Don't mess this up. It's Angelina-bloody-Jolie."

So I leave Angie standing on the doorstep and head off in search of the sweet stuff. Oh yeah. At last it's happening. I can hear the distant strains of an Al Green tune starting up. But no! I'm dealt the cruellest of blows. There's no sugar in the house. In desperation I offer her my girlfriend's emergency stash of sweetener but she's nonplussed and Angie leaves empty-handed. I wake up anxious and unsatisfied.

This dream has really unsettled me. All morning I'm plagued with questions. "Why didn't I invite her in? Why couldn't I have dreamt up some sugar?"

I decide to confide in my girlfriend. I tell her every detail: the white tank top; the sizzling sexual chemistry; the request for sugar; the lack of sugar. "What do you think this means?". Desperation rising, I repeat, "She wanted sugar, but I didn't have any sugar."

My girlfriend looks all serious and Dream-Analyst-like and there's a long pause as she appears to be considering the complex interplay of symbolism. Then she says, "I think it means it's your turn to go to the supermarket."

*I had the idea for this column at a Heather Peace gig and discussed it with a group of lesbian friends in attendance. Two found it funny and the rest were horrified so I thought it would make a good topic. My ex-girlfriend was hugely supportive of my writing and happy for me to write candidly about our lives, but I have to say this one was almost a deal breaker. To her enormous credit she thought it was funny and let me go ahead even though once it was published she felt lots of her friends would give her 'the look' – and she was right, they did.*

## Confessions of a Cock Encounter.

At the weekend I was enjoying my breakfast when cock flashed through my mind. It didn't last long; it was in and out before I could even take a slurp of my cappuccino.

I'd normally reach for mind bleach but suddenly I imagined my girlfriend with a hard on and, for a split second, I thought it might be a nice way to while away the morning. What's wrong with me? I'm a lesbian. We're talking about an erection here, not a trip to the garden centre.

It might be fun though, mightn't it? If it was attached to my girlfriend, all warm and ready to go? But I wouldn't want it to be there permanently, mind you.

Only occasionally, very occasionally. And please God no balls. Oh, and I'd have to know when it was coming. I can't bear surprises.

Does this make me sound straight? I realise I'm no gold star lesbian, but I thought I had at least made the grade. Has heterosexuality been lying dormant all this time ready to flare up at a moment's notice – like herpes?

When I first told my straight girlfriends that I was a lesbian they chimed in unison, "Won't you miss cock?". Nope. Giving up cock was a doddle, a cinch, compared to quitting cigarettes. But you know what they say, "Once a smoker always a smoker." Maybe I was over confident. What happens if cock's a habit I've never really shaken, and one day when I'm far too pissed at someone's wedding reception I end up scrounging the penile equivalent of a Mayfair?

The truth is I'm so much happier without cock in my life. It's nice not to be woken with a gun in your back at 5am because your partner's had a sexy dream about Mrs. Kravitz from next door. I cherish getting eye level with my girlfriend's crotch without fear of something trying to take out my tonsils.

I'm not unfulfilled either thank you very much. My vagina hasn't been abandoned like one of those disused Tube stations; no trains coming in or out for almost a decade. To labour an already terrible analogy, the train still goes into the tunnel and it's not what a train is made of that guarantees a good ride, it's the skill of the driver.

I look across the breakfast table at my girlfriend. Oh God. What if she thinks about cock? She has her eyes closed and her lips are firmly clamped around her last piece of Cumberland. What a horrible thought. It's enough to put a girl off her breakfast.

*I work in the often boysy world of advertising where innuendo is a part of everyday office life and banter. I wrote this because it made me smile that even though they knew I was a lesbian the innuendo directed at me was always straight in content.*

## Meatballs to Your Straight Innuendo.

Have you ever tried to eat a big meatball that's sitting in a pool of oil, off a polystyrene tray, while walking, with a blunt plastic fork? I imagine it's the sort of challenge that Bear Grylls eats for breakfast. I, on the other hand, am struggling to eat it for lunch.

Instead of rushing to my aid, the bloke with me, a big fan of the double entendre says, "Pop the whole ball in your mouth" and gives me a cheeky 'wink wink'. Everything is a rich source of innuendo where he's concerned, so this meatball is a gift. Suddenly it looks less like lunch and more like something I've seen recently on Embarrassing Bodies – and picturing Dr. Christian rolling it between his thumb and forefinger is a very effective appetite suppressant.

Don't get me wrong, I like a little 'fnarr fnarr' as much as the next person, but because the innuendos are generally hetero themed they don't always work. At a BBQ recently someone painfully laboured a joke about me getting some 'pork'. When you're a lesbian pork is just pork. If you're reaching for a double entendre, at least make it relevant. Maybe ask if I'd like to see your 'kebab'. We owe the memory of Jade Goody that much.

My friend is still goading me about the bloody meatball, so I decide to let him in on a secret. No one ever believes me, but I have a ridiculously small mouth. At first my dentist couldn't believe it either. She even called my girlfriend out of the waiting room to come laugh at me attempting to 'open wide'. My girlfriend said when she popped the mouth mirror in, it was like watching a postman stuffing a large Amazon parcel through a small letterbox. It's really tiny. I'd have to dislocate my jaw anaconda style to do what this bloke is suggesting.

Poking at my meatball, I confess, "It's too big. I couldn't fit it in my mouth. Just ask my girlfriend."

He looks at me in disgust. "Ugh. That's WAY too much information."

He clearly thinks I'm making an innuendo of my own, but I don't really understand what he's getting at. I'm a lesbian. Exactly what part of my girlfriend's body did he imagine me stuffing into my tiny opening? Her elbow? Can't he see that he's trying to crowbar a cock gag into my innocent small mouth comment, and it doesn't fit. Some innuendos simply don't translate.

I don't want to carry on this conversation any longer, so I spear my poor beleaguered ball and chuck it in the nearest bin. I've never really cared much for balls anyway.

*Ahhh sausages. I love sausages. No, really, I LOVE them. Can't get enough of their great big meaty goodness. Wait a minute. Stop laughing. This is a serious matter. What's so funny? Can't a lesbian declare her innocent love of wieners?*

## The Sausage Botherers: Dick Jokes That'll Make You Gag.

Being a carnivorous lesbian sometimes has its drawbacks. There are few things I enjoy more than a nice juicy sausage. I have yet to experience a personal crisis that a banger couldn't alleviate. And I've yet to enjoy a single meal that couldn't have been exponentially improved by the addition of a simple Cumberland. In my opinion it's one of life's last remaining pleasures. But, I've found that there's a group of people out there who refuse to let a lesbian enjoy her chipolata in peace.

This insidious group of characters, who shall be hitherto referred to as 'sausage botherers', are hell-bent on pissing on my frankfurter by drawing crass comparisons between the meaty feast I'm about to enjoy and a male member. They can't help themselves. And your average 'sausage botherer' isn't always easy to spot. You can be dining with someone you consider to be a most PC brunch partner, but one bite into your banger and they'll come over all Bernard Manning.

"I'll have the sausage please" is enough to get them crowing, "Ooh she loves a sausage." They'll invariably give me a little elbow nudge, and a Frankie Howerd-esque eyebrow raise just in case I missed the joke. Trust me I get the joke. It's really not that complicated. I'm a lesbian and you're making a cock gag. The reason I'm not laughing is because I don't find it funny. In fact, in my humble opinion this sort of sausage gag is the wurst excuse for humour.

Let's just get something straight here, I'm a sausage lover – end of. It's not code for anything else: I'm not craving a 'wiener', and I have absolutely no interest in entertaining a 'pork sword'. I just want a simple juicy pork sausage with cherrywood smoked, dry-cured bacon, made with prime British pork from pigs born outdoors and reared in airy, straw-bedded barns – is that too much to ask?

PART TWO

# COMING OUT

## Coming Out, Coming Out Again and Going Back In.

*I don't have the classic coming out story. I didn't actually come out, I just waited for people to guess. I took my 'friend' to every social event and family gathering for five years and eventually people suspected there might be more to it.*

*Since then, I've come out at the bus stop, on a fire escape, at the dry cleaners, outside a tube station, in Chippenham, and even on my own doorstep to the census man. Let me tell you, it's been exhausting.*

*I didn't officially come out until I was 30 and by that time it wasn't so much a ta-dah moment as "yeah tell us something we don't know." You could say I sort of leaked out gradually over a number of years, like the air from a run-flat tyre.*

## Coming Out: What Took Me So Long?

It took me a long time to download the fact I was a lesbian. For whatever reason the information required more bandwidth than I had available, so I was 26 when my brain finally stopped buffering and it loaded.

It seems obvious to me now that I was gay, but at the time I either ignored it, or reasoned it away. I'd tell myself that I wasn't a lesbian, I just happened to be a fan of Ellen's particular brand of neurotic situation comedy. I appreciated Martina Navratilova's 'athletic ability', but I wasn't a lesbian. I was a tennis fan. Okay, so I may have wanted to touch naked breasts with Belinda Carlisle, but didn't everyone?

My straight girlfriends imagined life as Mrs. Morten Harket, or pored over a penis named Ralph in Judy Blume's infamous book *Forever.* They wore out the heads of their parents' Betamax re-winding the sex scene from Risky Business. Meanwhile, I was being drawn, as if by invisible tractor beam, to the silky smooth voice of K D Lang, or the knee-wobbling intensity of Jodie Foster. But I had boyfriends, so I couldn't be a lesbian.

I was attracted to male TV stars, but it was always the female characters that I found most 'interesting'. I didn't read my feelings for them as attraction. I thought I wanted to be Juliet Bravo, Harriet Makepeace, or Christine Cagney. If I hadn't realised I was a lesbian I'd have gone into the police force.

Things changed the night I drunkenly kissed my friend in the bathroom at a fancy dress party. She was dressed like Uma Thurman in Pulp Fiction, and I'd come as Princess Leia. As my fake buns brushed against her fake bob I knew that what I felt was more than the sum of our combined synthetic wig static. Radiohead's No Surprises was playing outside the door as we kissed, and I felt my own heart fill up, like a landfill, with emotions I couldn't describe.

In that one instant I saw my lesbian life flash before my eyes: the school crushes, Kelly McGillis in uniform, the Aran love-fest that was Beth Jordache and Margaret, the Bad Girls box set, and Michelle Pfeiffer, on a stepladder, singing Cool Rider. For the first time in my life everything made sense – I finally understood why I liked Grease 2.

Sometimes I wonder if my life would have been different had I realised all this sooner. I think regretfully about all the time I wasted taking the scenic route. But the most important thing is that I'm here now, and being a lesbian is much better late than never.

*It was a real shock to me that coming out wasn't a cataclysmic one-off event that was done and over with. It was something I'd have to continue doing on an almost daily basis for the rest of my life.*

## Every Day is Coming Out Day.

Last week I came out to our greengrocer, right there between the carrots and the cabbages.

'"Your fella's getting well looked after," he would say cheerily every time I went in while picking over the courgettes, avoiding the bent ones. After two years of hearing the same line, I finally plucked up the courage to set him straight and said, "actually I have a girlfriend." I didn't have to, but I thought it might make things simpler. On reflection this might have been a mistake.

He clearly took the information on board, because today as I was reaching for a decent sized banana he said, "she's getting looked after well." I might be mistaken, but his catch phrase seemed to have a different ring to it this time and my choice of fruit took on a different significance.

No matter how many times I do it, coming out never gets easier. I always sound as though I'm apologising for something. "Sorry, I'm a lesbian. A pound of carrots please".

Far too many people on this planet still don't know I'm a lesbian. I have been telling people for years and I'm still barely through NW1. I'm worried it might take the rest of my natural life to get around to everyone.

I used to think coming out was something I would only have to do once, like having my appendix removed. Not the case. In reality it's more akin to heartburn; a daily irritation and discomfort. Wake up. Eat breakfast. Tell the person at the

Royal Mail collection office that you are a lesbian.

I first noticed the frequency with which I'd be required to come out when we bought our house. Between the mortgage broker, the lawyer and our new neighbours, we spent more time 'coming out' than moving in. The architect thought we were flat mates and was planning two equal sized bedrooms until we asked him to make one a master. He looked really puzzled and said "Which one of you is going to get lucky?". Should we tell him we both were?

I was okay telling my nearest and dearest; it was everyone else I wasn't prepared for: The Ocado man. Camden Council. My doctor. Countless friends-of-friends-of-friends. The gym admissions guy. The vet's receptionist (I think she was already on to us).

At last count I've come out at the bus stop, on a fire escape, at the dry cleaners, outside the tube station, in Chippenham, and even on my own doorstep (the census man).

IT'S EXHAUSTING!

Meanwhile, there's the greengrocer fiddling with the change in his apron pocket, keeping watch on me as I'm handling his root vegetables.

*Holidays can make me more wary than a French campsite toilet. This was one of my earliest columns and I'm pleased to say I've got the hang of it now.*

## Checking In, Coming Out: Is There No Escaping the Awkwardness?

Holidays make me nervous. Yes there is the promise of sun, sandals and San Miguel but to enjoy the holiday you must run the gauntlet of the hotel check-in. It is the lesbian equivalent of one of the 12 labours of Hercules.

Picture the scene. I'm standing at the reception check-in. It's hot and busy, a restless crowd has gathered behind us at the desk and Holiday Barbie is looking puzzled. Her eyes are darting between us and her computer screen as she says, "you ordered a double room?" It's started. Not a statement of fact, a question. Yes that's fine I say but it is not fine with her, she's going to right this wrong. She thinks we're a couple of straight chums away together. Two girls in one bed; that'll ruin our holiday. No, fear not, she will move us to a twin room where we'll be "far more comfortable". This of course is completely untrue, because after we've shoved the single beds together we will spend the entire time avoiding the sheeted crevasse.

I know I have about 30 seconds to make a stand. Now I'm wishing I had given them a clue when I booked. That was my first mistake. One of us is going to have to be brave and come clean. A whole hour's worth of arguing over who is going to man up is silently squeezed into 30 seconds of eyebrow acrobatics and some death stares. I lose. Now it's all about damage control. How do I retain the double bed with the least amount of embarrassment suffered to all parties?

Finally, I close my eyes and just blurt out "We're together". There's a moment's silence as the receptionist comprehends what she has just heard and flushes straight past tomato to a deep beetroot colour. The restless queue behind us is hushed. Now I know there'll be awkward silences in the breakfast room tomorrow as wives glare at their staring husbands and all you can hear is the silent gulping of tinned tomatoes.

Truth is, in order to enjoy a holiday you'll have to out yourself to at least 10 different people. It's an invasion of privacy I'm not sure I'll ever get used to. Perhaps even more infuriating though are the people that didn't get the memo. Enter two middle-aged lotharios later that night buying us drinks at the pool bar and asking "why don't you lovely ladies have boyfriends?"

*I'd had a number of boyfriends in the past and occasionally I'd bump into people who knew me from my previous life as 'straight Sarah'. I think when I first came out I felt the need to expunge that period of my life altogether. I'd obviously confused becoming a lesbian with entering the Witness Protection Program.*

## A Blast from My Heterosexual Past.

This week I was standing still for so long that my old life caught up with me. I was reunited with a friend from my pre-lesbian days when our two worlds – and trolleys – collided in Waitrose.

She said my name and it was as if she'd pulled the ripcord on my current life and sent me hurtling back to 1998. Back then, I dated my fair share of men but I could never work out why Mr. Right was only ever Mr. Just all-right. It was like playing an incredibly long Post-it party game: I had 'Lezzer' stuck to my forehead but it took years for me to figure it out.

So how do I tell this old friend I ditched Adam a long time ago…and I'm waiting for Eve (my girlfriend) to reappear any moment with some forbidden Cherry Garcia?

When I gave up men I should have been offered entry to the Lesbian Protection Programme. They'd have changed my name to Sue and moved me to a quiet suburb by now. It would have shielded me from running into people from my past and having to explain that it's not only my hairstyle that's changed.

My friend hasn't changed much at all. She still has a job in media, still lives in North London, and is still seeing Dave. In fact, now they're married. The only aisle I'm interested in, however, is the ice cream one. Where's my girlfriend?

I'm introduced to the child in her trolley, and in return I introduce her to the bumper pack of tampons and two bottles of Rioja in mine. (She probably thinks I'm having another drunken period.)

A warning light has come on. My conversational tank is nearing empty, and we are running dangerously low on small talk. I know that any minute now she'll ask, "So, are you married?". I am mentally scrolling through possible replies when she surprises me by saying, "You seem happier..."

She's right. I am happier – even supermarket shopping, early on a Saturday morning with a hangover.

Just then my girlfriend arrives and throws a tub of Ben and Jerry's into the trolley. As we say our goodbyes, I leave my past behind happy in the knowledge that there'll be ice cream in my future.

*As I was learning how to come out with confidence in new situations my dad was a revelation. I'd thought he would struggle with the idea of my being a lesbian, but I was very pleasantly surprised at how open he was, and how easy he found it to introduce me and my then girlfriend to his friends. He has a much better technique than me, take note!*

## Coming Out Lessons From My Father.

My dad has never been backward in coming forward, and it turns out he's not backward in coming out either – on my behalf. I've been known to hesitate, when introducing my girlfriend to his friends. I open my mouth, and "My girlfriend" is on the tip of my tongue, but like the words, I don't always come out.

Sometimes I decide that my being with a woman is need-to-know information. In my opinion, a bloke named Sven from my dad's golf club doesn't need to know. Other times it's down to cowardice, the desire to avoid what I anticipate will be an awkward silence.

But far from preventing awkwardness my reticence is generally the cause of it. It sets the wrong tone. Instead of being up front and coming out on my own terms, I'm either dragged out (through a series of questions), or worse, I accidentally fall out mid conversation – a lesbian malfunction.

This is possibly why my dad has assumed the 'coming out' duties when I'm with him. It's as if he's appointed himself the closet door bouncer, stopping me from entering. If he senses I'm not going to go through with it, he steps in and says with authority, "This is my daughter AND HER PARTNER."

There's no pause. No hesitation. He's up and 'outed' me before they've even got their coat off. I might hang back, stutter up a storm, or sound apologetic, but my dad is bristling with confidence. He removes any ambiguity from the situation and immediately puts everyone at ease.

Last week, however, his skills were put to the test when he invited my girlfriend and I to dinner with a very charming octogenarian friend of his who's a little deaf.

"This is my daughter Sarah AND HER PARTNER." No reaction. "This is my daughter Sarah (little louder) AND HER PARTNER." Nothing from his friend, but other diners were looking over at us. I would have been dying of embarrassment by this stage and probably bottled it, but my dad was completely unperturbed. He tried again, "I said my daughter (very loud) AND HER PARTNER". Thankfully, this time his friend heard it – as did the diners in the restaurant next door.

I've learnt a lot from my old man over the years: how to drive in snow, how to blag my way into a nightclub, and now how to come out with confidence. I have to take my hat off to him, because when it comes to coming out he's definitely the daddy!

*Unless you are everybody's idea of a 'stereotypical lesbian' (whatever that may be), or sporting a T-shirt that reads, 'Nobody knows I'm a lesbian', chances are at some point you'll have cause to correct people's mistaken assumptions about your sexuality. My advice? Do it quick, like ripping off a plaster, or it will be much more painful in the long run.*

## Actually, I'm a Lesbian: How to Correct Assumptions About Your Sexuality.

I'm enjoying a nice superficial conversation with my new client when things take an all too expected turn. He assumes I'm straight and refers to my 'boyfriend'. I politely but swiftly correct him with, "Girlfriend". Now I'm afraid I sounded like a pedant.

No matter how tactfully you do it, correcting someone's assumption about your sexuality is tricky. You sound like a schoolmistress. My client looks chastened, as if I'm going to ask him to write out 100 times, "I must not make assumptions".

We fumble through the next few minutes with him repeating, "GREAT. GREAT", the way a fire-walker might chant the words, "Cool Moss, Cool Moss" to focus the mind before he steps out onto hot coals.

My cheeks are burning from having corrected him. He's blushing from his assumption, and seeing him blush is making me blush even more. We're just passing the embarrassment back and forth between us, like a yeast infection.

If he was a stranger, I probably wouldn't have bothered. I'd have let sleeping lesbians lie. But I've got to work with him, and telling him further down the line would have been far more embarrassing. He'd end up resenting me for not being straight with him in the first place – even though that was the problem.

It's not the first time this week I've had to correct someone. My doctor asked if there was any chance I might be pregnant and not know. Not a sperm's chance in hell lady. I replied, "No" but she persisted. Was I sure? Was I absolutely positive? Sensing I was seconds away from peeing on a stick I told her I was positive – I was a lesbian.

People make assumptions because they're working with outdated stereotypes. They expect you to look a certain way and when you don't they don't see you coming. I get it. I've driven to London using my Dad's 1960s road map, and the M25 was indeed a big surprise.

Now I have to somehow salvage the situation. I decide to play the whole thing down for the sake of his pride. I tell him it's okay; lots of people make that mistake; it was probably my fault anyway, people never guess I'm a lesbian; how was he to know?

Wait a minute. Why am I apologising? Why am I making him feel better about his error. Now he's back on top. My strategy was flawed. Oh well, we all make mistakes.

*Even as an out lesbian I have found there are times and occasions when I really didn't feel like coming out to new people. I used to wonder if it was okay to just keep schtum sometimes, or would that be seen as letting the side down?*

## Is it Ever Okay to Go Back in the Closet?

There are moments in my life as a lesbian when I want back in. Times when I think to myself, "I'll just pop back to the closet a bit for a rest, and maybe a Hobnob, and come out again later. No one will know". This week, I had one of those moments.

I'm at a party with some people I barely know. It's late. I'm enjoying a drink and I don't feel like having a lesbian inquisition: *"Yes, I have dated men. No, I don't miss it. Neither of us is 'the man.' Bla...bla...bla."*

So, instead of being up front about my girlfriend, I do the sexuality sidestep and refer to her as my 'friend'. I haven't said 'friend' in so long it feels wrong, like the time my dad asked me to start calling him Jim.

In the days before I was out, I would introduce girls as my 'friend' to help me play it straight. I had 'friends from work', 'friends from the gym' and on more than one occasion 'friends of friends'. People didn't know if I was a lesbian or just very popular.

I thought I had come a long way since then, but here I am seven years on at a house party, smoking and talking about my 'friend' again. Scissor Sisters' 'Comfortably Numb' is playing in the background, and I'm wondering if I've I drunk myself back to 2004.

But this time it *is* different. I'm not pretending to be straight; I just didn't feel like coming out tonight.

Coming out to people you don't know can be exhausting. It's strangely intimate and not good content for convivial conversation. It requires too much explanation, like trying to give someone who's never seen EastEnders a recap of every episode in the last eight years.

The thing is, as I listen to myself talk, there's something missing. The confidence has gone and I'm not as much fun to be around. Like Clark Kent, I'm a bit shy and ordinary without my superpowers. I'm far more interesting as a lesbian.

As I leave the party and head home I wonder what my girlfriend will make of this. Then I remember: she'll have to forgive me, because that's what friends are for.

PART THREE

# FAMILY AND FRIENDS

## Performing a Lesbocism, Discussing Gender Roles and Role of Turkey Basters.

*In the words of Phil Mitchell this chapter is "awl abaht faaaaamily". Even if you've known you're a lesbian since you were knee-high to, well some knee-highs, it can take friends and family a little longer to adjust to the news. They may be upset or afraid that you're going to change into a completely different person, or that you're forfeiting your right to kids, or simply that you'll get a buzz cut and start wearing jackboots.*

*Family and friends can be an enormous support, as mine have been. But there were also some readjustments to make, and that led to many moments of awkwardness.*

*In the early days my ex-girlfriend and I hid our relationship from our parents. We preferred to think of it less as hiding something, and more that we just didn't think to mention it. From time to time, when my 'mother-in-law' enquired as to how my girlfriend was bearing up after months of sleeping on the sofa in my one-bed flat, she'd have to remember to appear suitably stoic and a bit stiff. When they came to visit, however, it was a different matter.*

## How to Perform a Lesbocism: Straightening up the House.

I urgently need to exorcise our house of all things 'lesbian' – in fact I need a lesbocism. My 'mother-in-law's' arrival is imminent, so we're systematically getting rid of any objects that could be construed as 'gay'. I've been having nightmares about her riffling through my drawers.

In the days before she knew that my girlfriend and I were a couple we had this ritual down to a tee. Bit by bit, like crime scene investigators combing a crime scene, we'd bag and tag any specks of deviance. One time we missed a Georgia O'Keefe print even though the labial-petals were staring us in the face, and as her gaze fell upon it she said "how in-ter-est-ing". She was probably wondering if it was art or a cry for help.

We might be 'out' to my girlfriend's mother these days but we don't want to leave evidence of it on the coffee table, we are not *that* 'out'. It's one thing to know your daughter is a lesbian, but another to see where the well-thumbed copy of *Sapphic Seductions* falls open.

A lesbocism begins by stripping lesbian novels and films from the shelves expelling Ellen, and casting out the L Word. I had no idea we even had so many lesbian films – where did they come from? We started out with Bound and High Art and they've multiplied like rabbits – which reminds me... anything phallic looking must be withdrawn pronto.

I refer to my check-list of ambiguous looking items for removal: *Two times bulbous shampoo bottles. Check. One times sheathed wine aerator. Check. Root vegetables various. Oh what the hell. Check.*

Why is it that in such situations even the most innocent of artifacts becomes sexualised? I bought my girlfriend's mother a case for her knitting needles once, and from the look on her face when I handed it to her, she clearly believed it was some kind of dildo protector.

Now, have I missed anything? Yes! I gather up the sets of underwear that are drying out two by two like a lesbian Noah's Ark. Nothing says your daughter's a lez like a pair of different sized bras nestled up together on a radiator.

This 'straightening up' also includes our behaviour while she's here. We've been practising our Laverne and Shirley happy flatmates routine all week. No kissing, no cuddling and definitely NO talking in tongues.

*My mum is very glamorous. I'm pretty sure she has never been mistaken for a lesbian. Except on one occasion when we were travelling together in Australia. We laughed a lot about this incident.*

## Mum's the Word: Hot Lesbian Couple Hits Port Douglas.

My first ever 'lesbian' haircut happened by accident. I've since read about girls getting a short haircut when coming out as a rite of passage, or later in an attempt to try on a different sort of lesbian look. Mine was neither. I was living in Sydney and although I'd had serious feelings for another woman in the past, at that point I was a long way from considering myself a lesbian. My haircut, a $10 special from a blokes' barber in a sleepy Australian town, was saying otherwise, however.

My plan was to get a bit off the length to cut down on the amount of time I'd need to spend in hostel showers. Instead I ended up looking like GI Jane without the muscles, more GI Jane lite or low GI Jane. You get what you pay for in this life, and my 10 bucks had gotten me a bloke's haircut just in time for the arrival of my very glamorous mum who hadn't seen me in 12 months.

"You've had a 'haircut.'" It's funny how four little words can carry so much subtext.

She seemed to give my new utilitarian cut quotation marks for emphasis, as if it wasn't doing a good enough job at standing out on its own. The way she said the word, slowly and deliberately, was her way of suggesting it wasn't so much a haircut as a statement, the equivalent of me bellowing the words "I'm a lesbian!" at everyone we met. But I'm getting ahead of myself.

During the trip she bought me a hat, a snug green number she encouraged me to wear every time we went out, which may or may not have been a coincidence. She had become paranoid about my getting sunstroke, even indoors. On occasions when I wasn't wearing the hat, if somebody else in our vicinity appeared to be looking at my hair, she'd break in and explain the haircut to them. A waiter would be in the middle of reciting the lunch menu and if his eyes flicked toward my fringe my mother would pipe up "It's just more convenient for when she's travelling. I'll have the crab special."

My hair was an ongoing issue. Every morning we'd get up to go and explore and I'd catch my mum looking at my haircut mournfully, probably wondering if it would ever reach my ears again in her lifetime. Never has two inches of hair been mourned for so long by so few.

A week into the visit, she'd finally stopped repeating the words "What have you done?" There had been no revelation about my sexuality so she'd started to relax and put my terrible haircut behind us. I was about to continue my travels around Australia and she was returning to the UK. Before she left we went out for a few drinks to a Sunday jazz festival in Port Douglas. While we were sitting outside shooting the breeze, a local reporter came to ask how we were enjoying our time here and we chatted and posed for a photograph, just another mum and daughter having fun on holiday.

On the day we left, the paper came out and we were very excited to see if our picture had made the society pages. Yes it had. There we were: Mrs Westwood and 'friend', according to the caption. My boycut and our apparent closeness had obviously confused the hack and here I was described in black and white as my mother's date. To her credit, mum totally saw the funny side, but we decided not to send a copy back home and instead keep it between us. Mum's the word.

*My mum has been amazing. She is always 100% supportive of me no matter what. I'm so grateful for that. I hope she doesn't mind me mentioning in fun that I like to think the only aspect of my being a lesbian that she finds potentially frightening is my dressing like one – whatever that means.*

## It's Christmas (But Don Me Not My Gay Apparel).

Christmas at home brings with it the pressure to dress festive which is code for 'girly': a party frock or a Christmas day outfit. I mustn't disappoint the line of uncles desperate to sing their annual chorus of, "Woo hoo look at you," or the more charmingly phrased, "You scrub up well," when I enter the room in anything other than jeans.

My mum, too, loves to see me, "make an effort". If my chosen outfit feels somehow lacking she will push a series of pashminas and scarves on me like some sort of crazed silk dealer desperate to get me hooked on accessories. "I've got a lovely bangle that will look nice with that. Look how nice. Just try it! Go on. Try it. Try. It." getting more insistent with each suggestion. Once it's on my wrist she'll admire it endlessly all night, "That suits you. Doesn't that suit her? That suits you. You should wear more jewellery."

My mum's mission in life, when I was younger, was to get me to dress in 'feminine' clothes. She went about it with the ardent zeal of someone utterly convinced that if she could only get me to stay in a dress long enough all would be well. Poor mum finally accepted defeat when I came home wearing a 'Meat is Murder' T-shirt I'd bought from Afflecks Palace; not the most feminine article of clothing I've ever bought.

If I'm caught musing over which black shirt to wear to the

Christmas nibbles the response comes back whip sharp, “Your sister’s wearing a dress.” The gauntlet has not only been thrown down it’s been colour co-ordinated. When I do put on a dress or a little floaty number, I’ll catch my mum staring at me with a faraway look in her eye. She’s like a contestant on Bullseye as Jim Bowen turns the board round to show them what they could have won.

Over Christmas and New Year I’ll no doubt attend a few dressy drinks parties, but ‘don me not my gay apparel’. No way. My family will encourage me to embrace the spirit of the season and wearing something more ‘cheerful’ and ‘Christmassy’– like a Santa suit. “I thought this was a celebration not a wake,” my dad will smirk. My concession to Christmas this year is wearing washed out festive grey rather than a darker shade of lesbian black. Okay so it’s not a pom-pom festooned bouclé red cardigan, but an All Saints sparkly skull T-Shirt is my nod to this sequinned season.

*I'm lucky to have an amazing sister and brother-in-law, and a gorgeous niece and nephew. I love those kids, but I've never wanted kids myself. I have observed that many of the older generation seem to believe that's because I'm a lesbian and I've therefore chosen a barren existence.*

## Cats, Kids and Turkey Basters.

My sister has just given birth. I'm excited as hell, but I'm also a little afraid that at all the get-togethers I'll be cast as the Patty to my sister's Marge.

When the womenfolk gather in the kitchen at parties, talking in hushed tones about the birth, I feel a little excluded. "You have NO idea", they'll say as they take another swig of Chardonnay. Au contraire friends, I did once stand on a piece of Lego in my stocking feet, so I do know something about pain.

I get the feeling that some people feel sorry for me; they see me as the poor barren auntie. They probably picture me kneeling down in my unfertile front garden, in full 'Platoon Pose', clutching dead Basil and crying, "Why. Will. Nothing. Grow."

Being a lesbian and having kids are not mutually exclusive. Still many people outside my North London bubble don't entertain the thought that I could choose to have children. "You'll be next!", they say to my niece's other (straight) aunts as they shoot me a look that says, "You'll be lucky!"

"Wouldn't you have liked children?" others ask, past tense, as if I had to make a Sophie's choice between The Candy Bar and Motherhood. Do they really think I've given up my womb altogether, letting it wither away like a dried porcini mushroom, in favour of 2 for 1 cocktails?

My mum will make well-meaning excuses on my behalf like,

"She has her cats". She says it in such a serious tone, that it sounds less like domestic pet ownership, and more like a vocation. People probably think my girlfriend and I are the lesbian Siegfried & Roy.

One Christmas, my dad grabbed the Conran turkey baster by the ball, and stole himself to ask, "Should I expect grandchildren?". Turned out he'd been reading The Daily Mail again. After a very pregnant pause he added, "Because it does happen, you know", before dropping the baster and mentally reaching for the mind bleach.

Some people, however, are interested in the 'ins and outs' of how my girlfriend and I would make a baby. They ambush me at the buffet for a blow-by-blow account. "But you can," (nod, nod), "have children?", (wink wink). To those people I just want to say, "Look buddy, we only just met. I'm not giving you the birds and the birds speech. Just eat your quiche and use your imagination."

*I think this was my first online column for DIVA. My 'in-laws' at the time were very welcoming and we were very lucky to be asked to spend time and holidays with them. They were always very generous to both of us. As accepting as they were, however, in all these situations there's always scope for awkwardness and humour.*

## Big Brogues to Fill: Assuming the Role of Pseudo Son-in-Law.

I've always prided myself on being 'good with the parents'. I'm the kind of girl that mums love and immediately draw to their bosom. With my girlfriend's mother however it was decidedly different – bosoms were treated as off limits. Before my current girlfriend I dated men, and I can honestly report that I was considered the perfect in-law. Not so with hers: within months I was less inlaw, more an outlaw. No matter how charming, I seemed destined to disappoint.

I don't think it helped that they thought that I had somehow managed to seduce her into this 'alternative lifestyle', an illusion my girlfriend did nothing to discourage. It was easier to allow her mother to believe that I was the lesbian temptress. It went nicely with my other titles; dyke destroyer of dreams (mum and dad's dream of a heterosexual daughter, that is), denier of grandchildren, or (in those days at least) white wedding massacrer. They probably imagined that she was all set to marry a rich, good looking – and male – banker until I showed up, putting her under my 'quirky' spell, and dazzling her with the offer of shared clothes and cats. Who could resist? She's only human after all.

The early days were the worst. Should they treat me like a daughter or a son-in-law? My 'father-in-law', for example, didn't know whether to flirt with me or give me a cigar, pat me on the back and talk man to er… man with me. Awkward. Apparently the solution was to hide out in his room listening to music – like a moody Tracy Barlow –for the entire duration of my stay.

My 'mother-in-law', a woman for whom hope springs eternal, held on to the belief that her daughter might eventually meet the right man and treated me more like a school chum on extended sleepover. The only time my girlfriend tried floating the idea of marriage she replied in excited stage whisper "…won't Sarah mind?" When she was informed that it was actually me she'd be doing the marrying with there followed a look of despondency.

However, five years on they are beginning to see advantages. My father-in-law is grateful that his position as patriarch of the family is not being challenged by a younger buck, plus he clearly believes that there's no obvious obligation to pay for a big wedding. And, as for my mother-in-law, she enjoys regular city breaks where she can have fun with 'the girls' and go out for sushi. We are reliably informed that men don't like sushi.

*This topic occurred to me one day after a single male friend confessed that he'd been ogling the breasts of a friend of his while she was breastfeeding. My friends have all wapped their breasts out in front of me at some point, but I've never looked because to me they were off-limits.*

## The Breasts of Friends: Are Some Boobs Not Up For Grabs?

In a changing room recently I was forced to navigate a very tight cubicle at the same time as a tricky social minefield. I was there to help a straight friend choose a new poolside outfit, but once summoned inside I found that she was 'between bikinis' and the space constraints meant we were now standing nose-to-nipple. When she cupped her naked breasts, offered them in front of my rapidly dilating pupils and asked, "What do you think?" I was like a dyke caught in the headlights.

Now, you might consider that having someone's chest thrust in your face is a good thing, but this incident got me thinking: lesbians, beware the poisoned charlies. It's all too easy to make a boob, you see. In this case, if I'm too rhapsodic in my praise, once removed from the highly charged atmosphere of Selfridges third floor she might start to wonder about all the other times I might have checked her out. She'll probably imagine me secretly appraising her on holiday, or grabbing a last tearful eyeful on the morning of her wedding and feel betrayed. But if I affect nonchalance, perhaps offer a little so-so hand gesture or shrug at her set she might feel slighted. I'm caught between a rock and a bra place.

I can't imagine the men I know grappling with the same kind of dilemma. They don't seem particularly concerned about setting appropriate boob boundaries. In fact you get the impression from some of them that they'd happily lean over the freezer cabinet in Tesco to cop a look at Aunt Bessie's shirt potatoes given half a chance. But as a lesbian whose own boobs have on occasion been the subject of unwanted attention I feel obliged to hold myself to a higher standard. You might say that I've drawn a bust-line in the sand.

The line I've drawn is this: that some boobs naturally flop into the category Norks That are a No No. Amongst the bosoms that I have sworn not to look lustily upon are those that belong to my therapist, my boss, or mourners at funerals, boobs that are blood related or breastfeeding beside me in Starbucks, emergency service boobs that are just doing a job, or a recently-been-broken-up-with-pair that are seeking comfort. Add to this, in theory, Her Majesty's royal rack. I would also include the breasts of friends, and in particular, boobs that go way back to school – the mams that matriculated with my own. Include the full roll call of tits that I went to university with and we're well into double figures.

Of course not every situation is so black and white – like an aged M&S bra there are grey areas. Immediate family is off limits obviously, but let's imagine, just for sake of argument, that we're talking about a distant relative, maybe a step-sister you rarely see, or a saucy second cousin. If the family fun bags in question are twice-removed from your own surely that would be sufficient separation? And what of other borderline boobs like, for example, those belonging to a friend's hot mum, or even, God forbid, the boobs that your lovely girlfriend inherited, yes ladies I'm talking about your own mother-in-law's melons. And while as a general rule I'd say that office boobs are a no go, what if they're not officially on staff payroll? I think freelance boobs are probably up for grabs, but feel free to make that call when you develop your own boob charter.

Yet even with such self-imposed standards firmly in place slip-ups do still occur from time to time. A great set of boobs walks by at a wedding, and buoyed up on bubbly it's simply impossible not to stare – then a second later Auntie Mable meets your gaze. In such cases the key is not to get busted. It's best to feign enthusiasm for her Monsoon ensemble, or simply offer to brush away an unsightly canapé crumb from her cleavage lest it ruins the photographs.

*I noticed that in interactions with my 'in-laws' they always treated me more like 'the man'. I guess they didn't want to imagine their daughter as 'the man', even though in truth neither of us was 'the man', because there was no man.*

## Talking Man-To-Man: I Talk Business With the Boys.

I'm a slightly inebriated English lesbian, out in the midday sun, chatting to a retired American advertising exec. He's a Don Draper type who's a friend of my girlfriend's parents. The 'girls' are inside, so he's bought me onto the deck of the beach bar to have a little man-to-man chat with me about politics and business. I'm now deeply regretting ordering the Cointreau float in my Cadillac Margarita.

When I'm with my girlfriend's family I'm often invited to shoot the breeze with the men folk, while my girlfriend is left to sit with the women. Curiously the situation is reversed when we're with my family. I put it down to the older generation needing to assign us traditional gender roles, and neither family wanting their own daughter to be 'the man' – even though 'the man' doesn't actually exist.

At first I found man talk quite difficult, but over the years I've become quite the master. You just have to remember to keep it curt and impersonal, and if in doubt, repeat yourself. In truth you don't actually need to say much, because it's more about the posturing.

"So," he says. "How's business?"

"Ah you know..." I reply. I add with a burdened sigh, "tough times." (If I'd had a cigar I'd have raised it to my mouth with dramatic effect at this point, but I didn't.)

"Yep. It's...."

The conversation has tailed off mid-sentence, because we're momentarily distracted by two attractive women wearing spray-on bikinis struggling to put up an unruly umbrella.

A few moments pass in silence as we continue to watch them, until he resumes, "Yep. It's tough alright."

We carry on staring through our sunglasses as the women bend over and dip into their bags, their bums in the air like ducks. One of the women is wearing a super tight silver bikini bottom, and I'm reminded of an old sofa cushion I once gaffer-taped to prevent the stuffing falling out. Don shifts in his seat a little and lets out a sigh. I'm guessing he's not recalling a gaffer-taped sofa cushion.

"So, how's business?"

"Ah, you know...."

We stare back at the bikini babes and take another sip of Margarita.

"I know," he sighs, "tough times."

*This one speaks for itself. It's just one of those funny faux pas that happens when you forget yourself and get a bit too comfy with the 'in-laws'.*

## The Time I Accidentally Described My Girlfriend as Slutty. To Her Parents.

I think I may have just inadvertently, in a roundabout way, inferred that my girlfriend is a bit 'slutty'. To her parents. As opening gambits go it wasn't my finest. I should perhaps have stuck with convention and congratulated them on the breakfast buffet with a simple, "nice spread."

They were talking about a new US TV show named 'Slutty Island', and I don't know why but I felt compelled to make a joke. Unfortunately, I chose "That's the way I like my women – slutty." I temporarily forgot that since their daughter is my girlfriend I'm therefore placing her firmly within this category. Even worse, when I realised it wasn't going to be funny I took my foot off the joke voice pedal so it faltered and came out sounding like a statement of fact.

It was a record scratch moment. Everyone looked to me for an explanation, including my girlfriend who went from not really 'slutty', to properly angry in under 60 seconds. It was too late to retract it and say, "Did I say slutty? What I meant was really smart and extremely chaste." The inference, albeit false, was out there. I could see that my in-laws were now processing the revelation that their daughter may be a little loose in the bedroom – like an IKEA bookcase.

To complicate matters further I'm not sure her parents have any concept of what we even do in the bedroom, let alone what activities might constitute 'slutty'. Come to think of it I'm not sure I know either, but her dad is now looking at me as if I am most definitely furnished with this information. And who can blame him? Leaning against the breakfast bar in my robe I've got a look of the legendary patriarch of the Playboy empire. Oh well, if the captain's cap fits.

Finally, after a heavily loaded-in-meaning pause my girlfriend's mother picked up the plate in front of her and said, "Can I tempt you to a fresh muffin". Steam was coming off it, so she was clearly hoping it would burn my mouth sufficiently to prevent me from casting further aspersions on her daughter. "Wow that's hot! Just the way I like my...." my words hung in the air, "...muffins."

*My 'in-laws' always let us sleep together and gave us a suite for our own privacy. I'm absolutely sure that they didn't put the cat litter trays in there on purpose, but I like to imagine they did because it's funnier that way.*

## No Sex Please, You're Lesbians: the In-Laws' Open Door Policy.

Sometimes I get the feeling that certain older relatives don't want us to have sexy time while we're staying in their house. They have an arsenal of tricks at hand to make sure there's no sex happening in their house – ever.

We are currently staying with one such relative who normally insists on force-feeding us pre-bedtime. She likes to give us something that will weigh so heavy on our sex drive that it nudges it into neutral, and we're incapable of doing anything but roll towards the bed and park up for the night.

This visit is no exception. She's outdone herself with an idea that's so fiendishly clever I'm not even annoyed, I'm actually impressed. She has three cats, and she's strategically placed their litter boxes in our en-suite. This stroke of passive aggressive genius means that we will have to keep the door to our bedroom open, to allow them access, for the duration of the trip. If that's not enough to curb our enthusiasm we'll also face multiple interruptions as the cat caravan makes it's nightly trek across the landing, through our bedroom, and into our bathroom, one after another, until they've all excavated their bowels. Cats are creatures of the night, so any nocturnal naughtiness will almost certainly be accompanied by their nightly ablutions.

Night one and sure enough just as we retire to bed the cats cometh. There might be a sound in this universe that is less erotically charged than that of a cat scraping its poo-laden paw on a tile that's two inches from your head, but if there is I can't name it. In fact, the cat in question may as well be burying my libido under a pile of cat litter. It's impossible to feel sexy in such circumstances – even Michael Douglas would struggle to be turned on with a cat log-relay passing by his head on an hourly basis.

But on the morning of the third day things appear to be looking up. I'm convinced that I have outwitted our host by becoming desensitised to the sound of the cat capers. I turn to my girlfriend and say, "I didn't hear anything! I don't even hear the cats any more, do you?" This is good news indeed. Then we look over to the bedroom door to find it closed. It had been closed all night. Moments later there's the anguished sound of a person who has clearly stepped in a pile of poo that has been deposited outside our bedroom door.

"Oh. Shit", says my girlfriend. I couldn't have put it better myself.

*This column was written in 2011 and reading it back I realise how far I've come. I used to be so stealthy and kept my relationship under wraps. All the pressure to do so was my own.*

## It's Christmas and We're Keeping Feelings Under Wraps.

Christmas is the time of year when you show those around you how much you love them. But for my girlfriend and I, it will be time for us to swap the open way that we live our lives in London for a chaste week sleeping side-by-side in my girlfriend's childhood bedroom.

My 'in-laws' accept our relationship, and welcome us with open arms, but there's an unspoken rule that we're not 'too out' in their presence. They want us to have ourselves a merry little Christmas, but not make the yuletide too gay. We'll have to keep our feelings for each other under wraps – like the presents.

There'll be no feeling around in stockings, no hoe hoe hoe-ing, and no impromptu kisses under the mistletoe for us. The best we can hope for is a stolen clinch in the garage, when my girlfriend is sent out to get more Diet Coke and I go to, "give her a hand".

We'll attend dressy drinks parties, but 'don we not our gay apparel', because my mother-in-law doesn't like to see us wearing dark shades of lesbian. She will insist on us sporting something more 'cheerful' and 'Christmassy'– like a Santa suit.

Such parties are a social tinderbox, a volatile mix of secrets and sherry. We must stick to the agreed 'story' of how we know each other, and not spark up potentially explosive small talk. One unguarded anecdote and our attempts at a low-key Christmas could go up in smoke.

What do you get the lesbian in your life that they can open in front of their parents? A gardening book. Anything that could be seen as 'inappropriate' must be opened in private. You've never experienced true fear until you've misplaced the Coco-de-Mer gift you bought your girlfriend, only to see her excitedly opening it in front of her expectant parents.

Christmas lunch will be lovely, but we must eat with the constant threat of Great Uncle Stan asking yet again why neither of us is married; at which point my mother-in-law will jump up like a scalded cat, to frantically create a diversion with the gravy.

Don't get me wrong, we're very lucky to be welcomed home for the holidays. I'm just dreaming of a Christmas when we can loosen our lesbian belts a notch or two, and let it all hang out.

PART FOUR

# RELATIONSHIPS

## That First Reluctant PDA, Dealing with Sibling Assumptions and the Little-Known Problem of Lesbian Bath Death.

*My first lesbian relationship began after our initial date and lasted almost 10 years. I guess I'm more of a cliché than I realised. We 'grew up' together, in the sense that we grew into our sexuality as a couple. We had both dated men in the past and were each other's first proper lesbian relationship. We weren't prepared for many of the differences that we faced being with another woman: the way people looked at us, being mistaken for sisters, having 'joint' periods, or clothes mix-ups that wouldn't happen in a straight relationship. That said everything else was exactly the same.*

*I used to be terrible about PDA in public, but these days I just throw myself into it. I'm often getting handsy in public.*

## Public Displays of Distraction: Unsure About PDA.

I think engaging in public displays of affection with my girlfriend is going to take a bit of getting used to – like the time I switched to Soy milk.

My issue with PDA is that it's just so…public. I'm not even talking about extreme 'get-a-room' exhibitionism, but just a little hand holding, or kissing. I watch with envy the ease with which other lesbian couples hold hands around Wholefoods, but when public push comes to shove I seize up.

When I'm with my girlfriend in public I feel as if every little gesture is amplified and sexualised. Even the most insignificant exchange feels like a huge declaration of homosexuality. A quick kiss, the removal of an errant eyelash, or even the ubiquitous hand squeeze all feel a bit shouty.

When my girlfriend attempts a sortie on my person in public I find ways to distract her. I'll spark up a new conversation, point at something, or make a bathroom run. I can turn a romantic meal into a West End farce (sadly minus the French maid's outfit).

But the truth is that all this distraction is becoming exhausting.

This weekend as we walked home from the pub arms swinging back and forth I knew that my girlfriend was preparing to catch hold of my hand. Just. One. More. Swing. Sure enough as our hands came close she made the grab. She got me!

Once I'd made the leap I actually began to enjoy it. It was quite liberating. I was a natural. What had I been worrying about? No one cares that we are two girls holding hands. No one is even looking. This is great.

I was just getting the hang of a little public affection, when I spotted an obstacle; a group of blokes drinking on the pavement outside a pub. They were directly in our path. We'd have to walk right through the middle of them to get home. This was a whole new level. My hand tensed. I wanted to let go, but my girlfriend held on tight.

I put my head down, took a deep breath, and braced myself for the comments I felt sure would come. But there were no comments. The gentlemen parted and allowed us through without a word.

I was elated. Wow all this time I'd been so anxious and people really don't care that we're lesbians. At that moment I overheard one of the blokes say wistfully, "Ah isn't that lovely. Can you imagine blokes doing that? Girls are so much better at showing each other affection."

Oh brother.

*I guarantee if you're in a lesbian relationship this will have happened to you at some point regardless of whether you look or sound alike.*

## "No, we're not sisters": Dealing With Sibling Assumptions.

There are very few certainties in life other than death, taxes, and the United Kingdom never again winning the Eurovision Song Contest. If you're in a lesbian relationship you can add one more to the list: the fact that random people will mistake you for sisters.

Passersby, shop owners, waiters, and so forth often mistake my girlfriend and me for sisters. They never let the fact that we don't look alike phase them – oh no – like a soap opera audience when a new actress turns up to play a familiar character they'll willingly suspend disbelief, even after they find out that we hail from different continents.

People sense that there's closeness between us, but "they're lesbians" is not their go-to explanation. A few years ago I was in hospital, morale was low from the combination of constant pain and beige food, and my girlfriend sat with me all day until visiting time was over. On my last day a fellow patient commented, "I wish I had a sister like that." Sister? Oh brother.

When people mistake us for sisters my first instinct is to correct them. But once the idea of 'sisters' has been introduced it feels a bit confrontational to pull the ripcord on their little sibling appreciation society and say, "lesbians actually."' They react as if you've deliberately tried to trick them with your little sister act.

Recently, while out shopping, a woman stopped us and said, "Oh my God, twins!" Twins? Eew! We immediately separated in an unconscious effort to highlight our differences – our romantic mooch reduced to mush. One minute I was looking at place mats, and the next someone was holding up a mirror to my narcissism. I found myself in Heals, in the midst of a deep personal panic. *We don't look that alike do we? Oh God, do I really just want to date me?*

People had now stopped to gawp at the 'twins', and the woman even called over her husband to confirm the sighting.

"Twins!" he confirmed.

God help the mister who was about to come between me, and my 'sister'.

"NO!" I replied horrified.

"But you look like sisters?"

"NO. We're not sisters."

No is usually pretty definitive, but in this case I sensed that more explanation was required. Everyone was looking to me to provide more information – including my girlfriend.

I know I should have just told them straight, but I also know it will get us out of there fast, with minimal fuss, so I lied and said, "We're very close friends".

The woman still wasn't buying it, "But you really look like sisters."

I turn to look at my girlfriend, and then look back at the shop owner and say, "We've obviously 'rubbed off' on each other."

*This was just a funny observation about adopting a pet name for each other and not knowing what worked. But if you spend any time with a group of lesbian couples it will be hauntingly familiar. And if you're a fan of Stevie Nicks, the phrase hauntingly familiar will be hauntingly familiar.*

## Too Many 'Babes': Finding the Perfect Pet Name.

At dinner with my girlfriend this week I had the Penne Arrabiata and a revelation: our conversation has become a chorus of Babe this and Babe that. We've started to sound like a broken Take That record.

"Babe, can you pass me the Parmesan." "More wine Babe?" "Thanks Babe."

The gap between the Babes is getting smaller. What if it disappears altogether and we lose our ability to string a sentence together? We won't be able to communicate with other people. We'll be forced to go and live in the woods, like watching the film *Nell* but in reverse.

It's already happening. We can anticipate the other's needs simply from the tone of the delivery. "Bay-Buh" means I'm hungry; "Ba-BBB" I want some attention; "BAY-bhhh" don't get mad, but I forgot to record Spooks.

It never used to be this way. When my girlfriend and I first merged we didn't know what to call each other, "Hey you" only gets you so far, so we defaulted to first names. We sounded less like lovers and more like primary school teachers taking a register.

We really struggled to find a pet name that was fit for purpose; something romantic yet ambiguous. Darling sounded too 'straight', Sweetie was too sugary, and Cupcake didn't last long (the downside of an edible name).

Then one day we were shopping in IKEA and between the KARENS and the OVANTAD's my girlfriend said "Babe what about this one?" We liked it so much – the word, not the vase – we took it home.

Babe ticked both our lesbian boxes: romantic when just the two of us, but we could still holler "Babe don't forget my nuts" in a dodgy pub without anyone raising an eyebrow.

But somewhere along the way we've gone from occasional usage to back-to-back Babes. It's become a serious 40-a-day habit. We have to start cutting down, and allow ourselves only the Babes we can't do without – the ones after dinner or at festivals.

Babe really ought to come with a health warning: this word is seriously addictive.

*This is the first of two columns I wrote about periods, I think because to some extent periods can rule a lesbian relationship. Either you've both got them at the same time, or they can seem never ending. I found it funny that my girlfriend at the time would ask about 'our period' as if even our cycle had merged.*

## "When are we getting our period?"

There was a time in my life when the word N' Sync brought to mind a boy band headed up by a blonde curly haired Justin Timberlake. Now it has an even more menacing connotation; the phenomenon whereby women who live together, menstruate together.

I am a firm believer that only one person in a relationship should menstruate at any one time. It's just simpler that way. When you are in a relationship with a bloke, periods remain shrouded in mystery. From the way that they suddenly appear in the wake of an unexplained rage to the unimaginable cramps and accoutrements involved. You only need mention your period and your bloke is off down the pub, giving you a wide berth, affording you extra care. "It's my period" is your Get Out Of Jail Free card. Play that card and you can shout profanities, eat what you want and turn down sex and parties. But not when you live with a woman, because they're in on it.

As if it wasn't enough that your 'free lunch' is taken away, you then start syncing periods as well as iPods. At first you hardly notice. They have their cycle, you have yours and in between there's room for some sympathy, some filling of hot water bottles, and even a little sex. Then inch by inch it happens every month one of you loses a day here the other there until boom, it's Armageddon.

You've gone from one discreet box of tampons in the cabinet

to stock piling. They're bulging out of cupboards and make-up bags, they're everywhere; on bathroom shelves, in car doors and bedside tables. You'll always find at least one in the fruit bowl and one is guaranteed to come torpedoing out of the arm of a coat pocket when you get to work. Then all of a sudden, they disappear, every last one and you'll be going through old handbags in a desperate search at 1am.

Hormonal rage and cramps are doubled. Every little gesture magnified twice over. There are arguments over who took the last tampon, arguments over who has worse pains, and over whose turn it is to fill the hot water bottle. Not to mention arguments over the stealing and eating of emergency chocolate. There are two fitful hot bodies tossing and turning at night, and twice the amount of annoying plastic tampon casings that stick to your socks when they've missed the bin.

I can't get used to the fact that periods, once a solitary pursuit, have become 'shared'. My girlfriend has even started saying things like "are we getting our period?" if we've had an unusually intense 'discussion' over what veg to serve with the tuna. If I seem a little more niggly than normal she'll say "it's because we're getting our period".

Well, I've had enough. I want my period back. I want it to have the space, and the respect it deserves. So, in this world of increased connectivity and synchronisation my period's taking a leaf out of Justin Timberlake's book. It's going solo.

## Out of Sync: A Miserable Menstrual Relay.

My period has suddenly stopped automatically syncing with my girlfriend's. I need to reboot my cycle. We've had 'the painters in' for what feels like an eternity without a break. The minute my period's done hers starts again. It is a bit like painting the Forth Bridge.

At first, our 'time of the month' happened at different times of the month. But the longer we were together the closer the dates got to each other. After a year of keeping my ovulatory independence I decided to go with the flow.

This so-called 'synchronised ovulation' is a quirk of evolution. People say it occurred so that the females were in sync with the Alpha female and ready for impregnation when the cavemen came back from hunting. I prefer to think of it as a way to allow all the chicks in the group to get it on with each other, while the blokes were off playing with their primitive tools.

A joint period, like a joint account, makes the monthly ins and outs easier to manage. You know exactly how many hours to allocate to being narky, bleeding, and eating Peppermint Aero, and what's left over for fun and games.

But suddenly we're out of sync. We've lost our regular rhythm and we're completely out of tune with one another. We're the pre-menstrual equivalent of a pre-school orchestra.

Meanwhile the house is bursting with sanitary accoutrement – it's a curse. I can't open a drawer, a bag or a coat pocket without a Lil-Let flying out. That's not to mention the ubiquitous tampon lurking at the bottom of the fruit bowl.

The worse part of this miserable menstrual relay is that it's seemingly never ending. As soon as I complete my leg I pass the baton on to my girlfriend for the cycle to begin all over again.

I've worked out that there's only a half an hour window each month when Aunt Floe isn't visiting, and it usually coincides with 30 Rock.

This interminable period has overstayed its welcome. It's become the last dinner party straggler lingering on too long at the end of an evening. We want to sneak off to bed, but it's cracked open the Pernod and put Stone Roses on the iPod.

Please God, just make it go. There's nothing else for it, I'll have to call it a cab.

*In the early days I thought the idea of taking a bath with your girlfriend was so romantic. When you are getting to know each other it's all candles and soap suds, and then after a few years the bathroom just becomes another place to have a meeting about domestic issues.*

## Lesbian Bath Death. The Beginning of the End?

I fear the idea of the perfect shared sexy bath time may have just disappeared down the proverbial plug-hole. We're now suffering from Lesbian Bath Death.

In the beginning of our relationship my girlfriend and I shared regular baths together. It was exactly how I'd imagined lesbian life would be; one big, soapy, soppy, sud fest. We'd spend many happy hours in the bath, candles all around, sipping wine, like something out of a Channel 5 movie. In our shallow little tub we'd indulge long, deep chats, and I remember thinking, "This is it, this is what it's all about."

But as the years went by, shared baths happened with less regularity. When they did occur old irritations began to take the shine out of the experience, like caustic soda on chrome fixtures. We'd bicker over who got the taps. Should it the first one in, or was it the right of the runner and instigator of the bath? We discovered that we were temperature incompatible; my girlfriend seemed to have developed asbestos skin and now insisted on having the water so hot it made lesbian soup.

Then we got our cat. The only cat in the world who prefers to come inside to use the 'bathroom' litter box. I'm not sure what it is about the sound of running taps, but it's like a double espresso on her digestive system. As soon as I'm fully submerged she hightails it in to relieve herself, with me stuck in the bath and helpless to stop her. I've tried locking her out. But it's not particularly relaxing having a soak when a cat propelled by an imminent bowel evacuation scratches desperately at the door.

Then, just when I'm getting used to the idea of floating solo my girlfriend surprises me by climbing in the tub. Maybe I was wrong and we can still enjoy a steamy Sapphic soak after all. I reach behind me to grab a tea light when she says, "We need to get that ceiling leak fixed". What? "And that tile is loose. And while we're at it we should really get this window seen too" We're not having fun times in the bath, we're conducting a wet inventory. Talk about bad news at bath time. Then I hear the door creak. It's the cat. Right on time.

*There's an equality and a lack of traditional gender roles at work in good lesbian relationships. I noticed that it also translated into snuggling. With guys you are normally the one being spooned because of size difference, but with women it's all up for grabs and it can occasionally result in a power struggle.*

## Snuggle Politics: The Flipside of Snuggling.

How do I love thee snuggling? Let me count the ways: I'm all for a bit of full frontal, I'm fond of a little spooning, and I love cosying up in 'the nook' of my girlfriend's armpit. That said, I have found that snuggling is not without its challenges, or indeed its politics.

Full frontal face-to-face snuggling, for example, is definitely not for the germaphobic. It requires well-practised, synchronised breathing lest you end up just recycling each others breath all night, air which ends up resembling the Kalahari-dry air you breathe on airplanes.

Spooning is less 'in your face', but instead of germs it breeds resentment. It's essentially an uneven nestle. Someone is always left under-snuggled. The larger spoon is exposed to the elements, and doesn't benefit from being tightly enveloped.

That's why, until recently, I believed that 'the nook' was the best way to snuggle. You know 'the nook' – it's that glorious sweet spot in between your girlfriend's chest and her arm. I like 'the nook' because, unlike the other two snuggle positions, I can see my girlfriend AND the television. It even has its own built-in padded breast pillow. That's snuggletopia.

But my girlfriend and I have suddenly reached a snuggling

impasse. She is claiming she's got a snuggle deficit stretching back over the last eight years; an unfilled cuddle quota. She wants to redress the balance and be the snuglee for a change. Now when we climb into bed there's a tussle – like two wasps fighting – for nook supremacy.

I don't mind letting her in 'the nook' briefly, but unlike her, I'm unable to fall asleep in that position. I have to be allowed to sleep on my side unencumbered. In my 36 years on the planet I've not mastered the art of sleeping on my back. I've tried, but it feels unnatural. I feel vulnerable, like an upturned tortoise or flipped over fly.

Tonight though, despite my plaintive reminders, my girlfriend has fallen asleep on me. Her head is lodged like a boulder in my nook, and I'm trapped; pinned to the bed. The more I wriggle to try to free myself the worse it gets. I can feel the panic rising. I crane to check the clock. It's only been 10 minutes. Great! I've got another 7 hours 50 minutes to reflect on just how much I love snuggling.

*Clothes mix-ups are a bit of a fact of life for a lesbian couple. You think you've put on five pounds overnight only to realise that you've just put on your girlfriend's bra by mistake. It's the kind of thing that doesn't happen to a straight couple.*

## The Wrong Trousers: Dealing with Clothing Mix-Ups.

It's been a bit of a stressful old time at work lately; so when I burst out of my last big meeting of the week I was flying high, and it transpired, flying low.

Apparently, while I was winding up to my big presentational reveal, my zip was winding down to reveal something else entirely – to a room full of clients. What rhymes with cringe?

I had been aware that the zipper had been struggling to pull itself together, but I had no idea it was just going to give up entirely – right then and there. Time to get a new zip – and a new client.

The very next day I organised an emergency zip replacement at the local dry cleaners so they'd be ready for the following night, because I was going out. But later that day, as I'm slipping into the mended jeans, I discover there's a problem. They're suddenly two inches shorter than when I took them in. They look ridiculous. I'm one sparkly glove away from being booked as a Michael Jackson impersonator.

My jeans are ruined. My evening's ruined. Everything is ruined. (I've lost all sense of perspective at this point).

My girlfriend hears the wails of despair from the bathroom and wanders in, "Why are you wearing my jeans?" she says – all casual – as if it's the most obvious question in the world.

Her jeans? Her jeans? I rummage around in the laundry basket, and find my jeans – dodgy zip perfectly intact. I have wrongly replaced a perfectly good zip in her jeans while mine lies broken. I'm wearing the wrong trousers.

I should probably point out that contrary to what people might think this is not a regular occurrence. My girlfriend and I don't share clothes. The fact that we're both women and of a similar size doesn't mean that we are all 'caring and wardrobe-sharing'. We're not. I haven't let so much as a belt out of my sight since my sister stole my beloved wasp belt for a whole term when I went to university. Mental note: I must get that belt back.

Instead of consoling me my girlfriend seems to think it's funny; yet another testament to my rubbish ways. She thinks it's 'priceless', but with another zip replacement it's actually going to cost me £20. It's not fair. It feels like a lesbian tax on indistinguishable denim.

Later that night as we are at the party, I notice that the laughter has stopped. "This zip keeps coming down" she says turning her back to me as she hoists it up again, "It never used to before, but now it does."

What never came down now comes down.

Don't you just love a bit of zipper karma.

*I think the subject of this next column is an issue that is probably shared by some straight couples. Not convinced? Just imagine the shower plughole at Anita Dobson and Brian May's house.*

## The Mane is the Bane of the Long-haired Lesbian Couple.

I've got a bone, or a strand of keratin, or whatever the hell else it's made from, to pick with hair. The mane really is the bane of the long-haired lesbian couple. If you have long hair, and you enter into a relationship with another longhaired lady you're sentencing yourself to a lifetime spent removing hair from off the floor, only to have more grow back in its place and for the cycle to repeat itself. It's the kind of backbreaking eternal hard labour that makes King Sisyphus's boulder pushing punishment from the Gods look like a little light medicine ball training.

I love long hair. What's not to love about long flowing locks – when they're attached to a head? I take my hat off to hair that's in active employment keeping sunburn at bay, or keeping heat in, or even hair that's just there to look good. It's detached hair that I have the beef with. Hair that's given up being head furnishing, and rather than disappearing quietly into the night, or having the good grace to drop off while we're out and about, chooses to stick around the house in cliquey clumps tormenting me.

Why is it that hair that was once admired on a loved one's head takes on a far less savoury appearance the moment it's shed? When, for example, you're hauling it out of the washing machine tangled up like a century-old fishing net, or when you open the door on a balmy evening and the breeze sends a giant hairy nest skittering across the floor like tumbleweed. One minute you're complimenting its silky smoothness, and the next you're staring in morbid disgust as the cat strolls by with a clump of the exact same hair stuck to its arse.

Imagine if L'Oreal featured a luscious-locked lesbian in their advertising instead of their usual string of straight celebrities. She'd be swishing her mop about in the foreground saying, "Because I'm worth it" – meanwhile her long-suffering partner would be on her hands and knees in the background, out of focus, picking at least eight separate hairs off the high pile rug.

When there are two lots of long hair swishing about the joint there's so much hair to deal with you can forget doing anything else with your spare time. There's no time for romantic walks in the park, or cinema dates. You now exist solely for the purpose of harvesting strewn strands. You'll find them clinging to the bottom of socks, or fashioning themselves into hair pillow cushions. Hairy clothes means factoring an extra 20 minutes of 'getting ready time', because you now need to perform the very necessary ritual of going over every square inch of each other's bodies with the lint roller before you leave the house.

My fear and dread of hair means I'm easily seduced into buying all sorts of hair-gathering gadgets. If it promises to pick up hair in a jiffy – you name it, I've got it. But the trouble is nothing works. Microfibre mops are the worst. As far as I can fathom all they do is take the hair for a spin around the floor and leave it in a sodden mess beside the bucket, and thanks to the addition of hot water and cleaning chemicals, it's laminated onto the floor forever. Have you ever tried to pick up wet loose hairs from a floor? It would make a deceptively simple challenge on that game show The Cube. Imagine Schofield ratcheting up the tension as the nation watches some poor contestant failing to drive a few sodden strands into a waiting dustpan.

God, this cycle of hair growth and loose hair is relentless. If you've ever seen a child cranking Play-Doh hair out of an inanimate toy head you'll know exactly what I mean. We need to nip it in the bud and get a buzz cut. It would be lovely to get through a meal without catching sight of a discarded human hairball mid mouthful, and coughing up a lung.

*No matter if it's cats or kids, when a third element enters the relationship the dynamic shifts. It might be imperceptible at first, then unmistakably, three is a little too much company.*

## Feline Interruptus: It's Sex or the Cat.

My girlfriend and I have been reminiscing about life PC (pre-cat). It was a simpler time. Just the two of us in bed together. Alone. Our sexy time wasn't accompanied by a cat commentary, and we didn't have to negotiate a large feline parked at an obtuse angle on the duvet between us. Since we got the cat she has made it her mission to interrupt any spontaneous loving at every opportunity. I get the feeling she really doesn't want us to have kittens.

The other night I was putting the moves on my girlfriend. I had a nipple in my mouth and it was going well until I glanced up and inadvertently made eye contact with the cat. "Meow". She sounded a little appalled. I was determined not to become distracted from the job at hand so I turned my attention back to my girlfriend. "Meeeeoooowww". "MMEEOOWW". The cat became more and more insistent until I had to pet her again to keep her quiet. Every time I tried to disengage my hand she let out a loud "Meow". So I was left, left hand on left boob and right hand on cat's head as if engaged in a Special Edition of Lesbian Twister.

The problem is that our cat is a third wheel. She likes to get involved in a little fur on skin action. She nuzzles up so ridiculously close to my naked body that she increases my overall body temperature by 50 per cent just by being there. Then I'm pinned in one uncomfortable spot unable to engage in any activity because any move I make will have a knock-on effect on the cat. If I move an inch she lets out a very irritated "MOOOW" and pointedly gets up, forms a ridiculously tight turning circle, and plonks down again in the exactly the same spot.

Our cat also loves to watch. She has, it turns out, a slightly seedy penchant for voyeurism. It's a bit awkward doing the do with the cat looking on. It just feels wrong. So these days we wait until she's dead to the world, sleeping in her bed, and when we spot the gentle soporific rise and fall of her breathing we sneak off to the bedroom. But by the time we get there she's somehow managed to get there ahead of us. Worse, she's plonked in the middle of the bed, reclining against our pillows, legs casually aloft, and is discarding a small poo remnant onto our new Cath Kidston bedding.

She has no sense of boundaries. It's no good leaving a towel on the door to signal our intention. She'll happily force her way, from the foot of the bed, under the duvet, until she reaches my girlfriend and I mid snog, at which point she'll flip open her head in a ridiculously over the top yawn and blast us with the libido crushing smell of her rancid tuna breath.

For someone who doesn't move much all day she comes alive at night, gamefully jumping onto the bed and clambering across boobs and bladders. Try to turn her away, or turn your back on her and she'll nuzzle her wet snout into your warm back, drag a claw down the length of your arm with increasing persistence, or worse still shake her head and cover us both in a light spritz of cat spit before settling down to snooze again. Talk about buzz kill.

Then the other night, as we were getting jiggy with it, the cat arrived on cue, but acting uncharacteristically nonchalant about the whole thing. Instead of interrupting us she was behaving aloof. She wandered into the bedroom, got cosy on a pillow on the floor, and ignored us. A breakthrough! We were imagining things returning to the way they were before. Just us. No interruptions. Just... then we heard it, a terrible frightening sound that could only be described as a rasping death rattle. It was the cat snoring.

PART FIVE

# OUT AT WORK

## Playing The Pronoun Game, Introducing Imaginary Boyfriends and Daring to Dress Femme.

*Coming out at work can be a difficult decision for any lesbian. I never actually told my work colleagues that I was a lesbian – I was too embarrassed to say the word so we just played a game of charades until they guessed; one word, three syllables, sounds like thespian. Even now, many years on, I'm still not out to everyone in the same way; there are levels of 'outness', like privacy settings on Facebook. I'm only a little bit lez with Brian in accounts but I let it all hang out with the girls in the office.*

*I didn't come out at first because I didn't want to risk being labelled as 'lesbian Sarah', or to have people think of me in a different way. The problem is that if you are not yourself at work, keeping up the pretence is a second job.*

*Chances are, if you are a lesbian you'll have played the pronoun game. I have backed myself into a conversational corner on numerous occasions by running out of pronouns. Back to the wall, I once even considered referring to my girlfriend as 'it'.*

## The Conversational Cul-de-Sac: Playing the Pronoun Game.

I hadn't intended to come out to my client at dinner while she had a mouthful of amuse bouché – it just happened.

It is not that I mind clients knowing I'm a lesbian, I just don't want to be the one to tell them. It's not conducive to small talk; nothing is more guaranteed to create conversational whiplash than announcing that your partner is actually a she. It's always out of the blue for them, as if they've asked you where you live and you've replied "I decapitated my childhood rabbit".

This week the situation was made worse because the client in question was a French woman. French women always strike me as completely man-centric; they might be adventurous eaters but women are always off the menu as far as they are concerned.

On this occasion difficulties arise almost immediately. "What does your partner do?"

Here we go. Prepare to enter pronoun purgatory.

"THEY work in the city". I felt like I had given those four letters pantomime-esque emphasis.

Her questions are relentless – I am now playing a sort of high-octane pronoun ping-pong. As quick as she can ask questions I'm batting them back just as fast with a 'they' or 'we'.

"WE went to Spain. THEY get on well with my family. WE

both like cooking. THEY take care of the garden."

It was exhausting; a linguistic Olympics.

Then, after four successive THEYs in a row I realise I'm running out of pronouns.

Oh God, I have backed myself into a conversational cul-de-sac. Unless I refer to my girlfriend as 'it', I'm going to say 'she'.

My lips have formed around the 'Sh' but my confession is temporarily interrupted by a waiter, offering some veal tartare. The client pops one in enthusiastically but I refuse (I don't eat veal and I'm about to drop a she-bomb).

I try to sound casual "SHE's, ..."

She is staring at me in abject horror. "You're not a...'

Oh God, she's not going to say it. Is she? I brace myself.

"Vegetarian?"

What? Did she hear what I just said?

It turned out she had indeed heard but her concern over my vegetarianism had eclipsed my big lesbian reveal. Relieved to hear I wasn't 'one of them' my vegephobic was happy and order was restored.

*This column is about Peter. He was my Sacha Fierce, my Jo Calderone. Unfortunately, as is often the case with such things Peter got out of control and became my slightly inflated alter ego.*

## Alter Ego Trip, or Why it's Not a Good Idea to Invent a Boyfriend.

Until very recently there were three people in my relationship: my girlfriend, myself, and a man named Peter.

My girlfriend, who worked in The City, was closeted at the office, not an easy feat when it's open plan. One day her colleagues put her on the spot to name her partner and she panicked. She wasn't ready to come out over an Excel spreadsheet, so completely uncalculated she lied, and produced Peter.

Peter became my alter ego. By night I was Sarah Westwood, Rubbish Lesbian, but by day (at my girlfriend's office), at least, I was referred to as Peter.

At first I was a little put out by her choice of 'Peter'; wasn't it a pet name for a penis? Apparently, she was desperately racking her brain for a man's name, Peter popped up, and she just grabbed it with both hands.

Talking about Peter made my girlfriend feel less like the office lesbian, she was finally one of the girls. At lunch when the subject of fellas came up she could play with Peter, and join in with a faux moan about his shortcomings.

She also used Peter as a way to get out of things she didn't want to do. I would never have stopped my girlfriend from attending work socials, but Peter had no such inhibitions. If he had just come back from being away he'd stop her going out for drinks – talk about an alter ego trip.

There's playing the pronoun game, and then there is creating a complete storyline for a boyfriend who doesn't exist. While the former is a simple sidestep, the latter is completely freestyle, and far more exhausting.

Soon my girlfriend was working overtime – on Peter. She was continually having to make excuses for his absence: Peter's Christmas party clashed with hers, Peter was on a rugby trip, Peter wasn't feeling well. He became more and more demanding; it was hard to keep it up.

Perhaps unsurprisingly, people began to tire of Peter, and his elusive and demanding ways. My girlfriend decided that the time had come to give this alter ego the heave ho. Poor Peter, he never even saw it coming.

I'm pleased to reveal that she has since moved jobs, and is out to her new work colleagues. She can finally be herself at work, and I'm thrilled that I no longer have to answer to Peter.

*I don't think this is so much a lesbian thing as a woman thing. People make different assumptions about you when you wear a dress. In particular, there's something about dressing femme that makes blokes come over all funny.*

## Does my Bum look Gay in This? Wearing a Skirt to the Office.

I envy people who are able to receive compliments graciously. I can't take a compliment at all. If someone throws me a compliment I shoot it down in flames. You like my top? It's M&S. I bought it ages ago. It was cheap. I don't like it much. It's too small for me. Then we stand awkwardly in the fallout, particles of compliment raining down, until the person makes their excuses and moves on to talk to someone with more evolved social skills.

If I do get a compliment it usually happens when I'm having a femme day. If I rock up to work wearing my hair down, with a bit of lippy on or wearing a skirt, my female colleagues will inevitably say, "Oooh, you look GOOD today." They're giving me their unsolicited approval for trying on a 'straight' look, as if I've just emerged shoulders hunched from the changing room and asked, "Does my bum look gay in this?"

Male colleagues, on the other hand, seem to mistake my little forays into more feminine attire as a for a cry for help, evidence that somewhere inside there's a straight person – possibly stuck in Spanx – trying to get out. I have tried to explain to them that it's not the clothes that maketh the lesbian…it's the sight of Kylie spinning around in hot pants.

I wore a dress to a meeting this week and, sure enough, as I walked through the door a bloke in the office called me over to him, as an owner might receive their dog returning triumphant with a ball. “You’re wearing a dress! Well done girl!” I was quite relieved when he didn’t ask me to roll over so he could tickle my tummy.

“You’re wearing a dress”. Oh, here we go. This always happens when I wear a dress. People feel compelled to remind me of that fact, just in case I hadn’t noticed – as if it’s ketchup on my chin. I’m glad to hear I am in fact wearing a dress, because from the look on his face I was beginning to worry that I’d left the house without it.

It’s a tricky statement to respond to. You’re wearing a dress? How do I reply to that? I can’t say, “Thank you”, because technically it’s not a compliment, it’s a statement of fact. It’s almost a compliment. Actually, it’s an adjective short of a compliment, but who’s counting? Somehow we stumble into a rather perfunctory flirting session. He knows I’m a lesbian, but he’s battling millions of years of evolution at seeing me in a dress. Then just as I’m about to leave he says, “You look good in a dress”. Oh no. There it is. The compliment. I know I must accept it graciously and move on.

“Thanks.” I splutter, “You too.”

*I used to dread having to come out anew to every person who joined the firm. I think there's a lesson in this one about over-thinking things.*

## Everybody Out: Accidentally Coming Out to the New Girl During a Fire Alarm.

I accidentally came out to the new girl at work this week during a routine fire alarm. Someone shouted, "Everybody out", and I took it literally.

I'm not fond of telling new members of the team that I'm gay. It has nothing to do with how I feel about it, but I feel responsible for managing their feelings. Coming out to new people at work creates a moment of premature intimacy. It sounds like I've made a personal revelation akin to, "My husband doesn't understand me", when we're still at the level of "are you a tea or coffee person?". But if I don't tell them, I run the risk of them making assumptions and then feeling foolish – it's a social minefield.

I've learned to delegate the task of telling new people to my friend. Her technique is quick and painless – like ripping off a plaster. One lunch hour during their first week she'll sidle up to the new person and say, "Sarah's a lesbian". She's in and outed me before the ping of the microwave signals their jacket potato's ready.

The fire alarm is sounding, and I'm standing on the pavement talking to our new girl. My own alarm bells are ringing. I must not out myself in this chat. I must stick to small talk about the weather, the Olympics, or the Olympic weather.

"I saw women's beach volleyball last night." What am I saying? Women's beach volleyball?

"I hope you got to see the men's match too?"

Men play beach volleyball? That's news to me. But then I do vaguely recall someone telling me that I was missing a men's match as I stood in line for more rosé. "No, we didn't see any men play."

"Oh well at least your boyfriend enjoyed it." There's a sudden pause and she says, "Oh sorry. Do you have a boyfriend?".

I could say, "no" and leave it at that. It wouldn't be lying. It's a partial truth. I'm hurtling towards a conversational crossroads and I can't decide which way to turn.

"Actually I have a girlfriend." I'm now rowing backwards faster than Sir Steve Redgrave in an attempt to own the moment, and be cool and confident.

"Oh, I'm sorry."

Is she sorry that I'm gay, or sorry that she'd made the assumption that I was straight? The question mark is still hanging in the air when the alarm stops. We're saved by the bell, and as quickly as I had come out I head back in.

*I firmly believe in being out at work, but then I am lucky to work in a creative industry where people are perhaps more accepting. Perhaps. I know it's a tricky decision to come out at work but it does make life a lot easier.*

## Being in the Closet at the Office is Too Much Like Hard Work.

If being a lesbian was like joining a gym – and by that I don't mean that you'd pay a monthly subscription and never make use of the facilities – then today I met someone who would classify as a 'peak' member. She's lesbian fo sho, but only first thing in the morning and after work. The rest of the time, as far as her colleagues are concerned at least, she's straight.

Being in the closet at work isn't easy, especially if it's open plan, because there's nowhere to hide. I didn't actually come out and tell my work colleagues I was a lesbian. We just played a sort of drawn-out game of charades until they guessed - one word, three syllables, sounds like thespian.

I was worried that people would start treating me differently once they found out. The girls might not treat me as one of the girls anymore. I might not be invited to lunch with them to digest the full horror of their fellas' football injuries along with my baked potato. I wasn't ready to be one of the blokes either, and spend every spare five minutes I had propped up against the photocopier talking about the new girl's boobs.

In fact the only person who treated me differently was the HR lady. I had never been on her radar before, but all of a sudden she was wary of me. She seemed to view the term lesbian as shorthand for office activist. She'd come to me to apologise for any delay in the arrival of the ergonomic chairs, or for the lack of gel wrist rest mousepads as if I was going to whip my colleagues up into a frenzy about the dangers of repetitive strain, because that's what lesbians do – they make unreasonable demands, such as for the key to the meeting biscuits cupboard.

My boss was happy. I think the news that I was a lesbian upped their diversity quota by 100%. He suddenly became interested in my life. In one particular meeting the client was wearing a blazer with her jeans and he nudged me and whispered, "Is she one of yours?". What's that? A Zara shopper, or simply another fan of this classic look?

Leap forward two years and I'm completely out to everyone I meet, but not in the same way. There are levels of 'outness'. I have different privacy settings, like Facebook. I'm only a little bit lez with some people, but I let it all hang out with others. I think it's important to be out at work if you can, because it's not easy living a double life. It's like having a second job, and no one wants that. One job is hard enough.

*I think there's almost a sort of assumed embarrassment when undressing or sharing a bed with a straight girlfriend, or in this case colleague. In reality it's just like sharing a bed with anyone you don't know very well. It has little to do with sexuality and more to do with intimacy. I think there's an added awkwardness on my part because I worry that they might think I fancy them just because I'm a lesbian.*

## One Small Room at the Holiday Inn: Sharing a Bed with a Colleague.

I turn up late to a hotel with a female work colleague to find there's only one room at the inn – a small double. Since I was in charge of the booking it's entirely my mix up. We're going to have to share it, or 'bunk up together', as my mum would say. The colleague in question knows I'm gay and it's never been a big deal, but I can tell that the prospect of being horizontal together for twelve hours, in a room with a travel kettle, might change that.

The easy conversation we were having at the desk petered out pretty quickly with the words, 'one small double', and now we're in an awkward stand off. I'm worried that if I appear to be too fine with the situation she might think I made this mistake on purpose and it's a seduction ploy. So I've adopted a theatrical look of annoyance. She, on the other hand, is trying to appear completely unconcerned in an attempt to avoid being uncool. "I'm fine if you're fine?" "I'm absolutely fine. If you are?" "I'm totally fine – if you're fine." "It's all cool with me." This tedious display of nonchalance continues for 10 minutes until the receptionist tires of it and throws a key in our direction.

When we get to the room things go from bad to worse. It's tiny. To be in this room is to be on the bed – it's basically a bed in a box. It's getting late, so the first hurdle we face is transitioning into our pyjamas without nakedness. If you've ever tried to do this you'll know it's basically like auditioning as a Quick Change Act for Britain's Got Talent – you're out of one outfit and into another in seconds. But in my experience when you try to remove clothes quickly you're more likely to get a foot caught in a trouser leg and be hopping around with your butt hanging out; not to mention the difficulty of attempting to remove a bra by dragging it out through the very small tight opening at the top of your blouse.

I decide the best course of action is to take my leave, and my pyjamas to the bathroom so she can change in private. But once I've changed I'm trapped in there wondering how long to leave it before I come out. I don't want to barge out and catch her with one leg in and one leg out of her pants, or worse, so I'm mentally estimating her undressing time. I give her 10 minutes – enough time to have changed and boiled the perfect egg for good measure.

Then it's bedtime. I don't want to negotiate which side of the bed she prefers because it sounds like I'm trying to establish a routine. Instead I get in quickly, feign a yawn, and then lie rigidly. I pretend to be asleep for an hour, clutching onto the edge of the bed with my fingernails so that I don't accidentally roll into the middle and touch bottoms.

The following morning as I re-enter the world I'm temporarily discombobulated – I'm no longer the same side of the bed and I'm being spooned. Good God. How do I slip the spoon to save her the blushes? It's like that scene in Indiana Jones – I need to replace the weight of the statue with a bag of sand. I'm just reaching around for a 5ft 7inch bag of lard when she awakens. There's a brief moment of silence while she gets her head around the logistics. Poor thing. She's going to feel terrible because technically the spoonee in this situation takes the lion's share of the embarrassment. But as I slink into the bathroom I catch her looking at me funny and a thought occurs to me: she thinks I backed into it.

*A learning curve for me was how to deal with the office Christmas party. Women getting tanked on free booze and regaling me with their lesbian antics, and men forgetting I'm a lesbian and going in for a Christmas snog.*

## The Office Christmas Party: Suddenly Everyone's a Lesbian.

Ah, the office Christmas party. All year round the fact I'm a lesbian goes largely unnoticed. It's of little interest to my colleagues. But there's something about that heady mix of free bar, cheesy venue and afternoon drinking that brings out the lesbian fascination in everyone. It's open festive season on lesbians.

From the moment I hear the till ring and Noddy Holder boom, "It's Christmas" I'm in fear of being ambushed by those desperate to reveal their brushes with lesbianism. Last year one colleague sat down sloshing a martini and said, "I don't think I've got any lesbian stories." Praise be! Then she followed up with, "I fingered a girl at school once. Does that count?" Dear God, can't a woman eat a vol-au-vent in peace?

The annual work Christmas party is a vortex that draws in and destroys every scrap of common decency and social etiquette, as well as everything you ever held to be true about your work colleagues. When else would you find your entire company grinding on the dance floor as if their lives depended on it at 2.30pm on a Wednesday afternoon?

The very fact it's a Christmas party seems to excuse any amount of terrible, out of character behaviour that follows. You can behave moderately for 11 months of the year then throw up in your handbag, snog the face off a work colleague, and order a round of flaming Sambuca at lunch, all because 'It's Christmas'.

All bets are off.

My dread of the Christmas party begins as soon as the hangover from the current one wears off. Blokes think that the arrival of the Christmas party means I may be ready for an epiphany of my own. One glass of cheap fizz and they convince themselves that I'll be interested in a snog – because after all, 'It's Christmas'. One year a married guy followed me into the loos and requested a kiss. When I said, "You do know I'm a lesbian don't you?" He replied, "I don't care". That may be true mate, but I MIGHT.

The response of most straight women I work with to the idea of lesbians is normally, "It's great you're a lesbian and everything, but I can't imagine it myself." But cometh the Christmas party, they form a patient queue to the booth I'm ensconced in, as if it's the line to Santa's grotto. Then scooching up next to me, until they're practically sitting on my knee, they tell me that what they really want for Christmas is to kiss a girl.

It's the horribly confessional colleagues I find the most challenging. Do they think I've got the power to absolve them of any past lesbian action over a mulled wine? I don't want to hear it ladies – any talk of fingering should be reserved for the buffet.

PART SIX

# LESBIAN STEREOTYPES

## The Usual Suspects Including Sporty Types, Trips to IKEA and the Obligatory Cat.

*When I first realised I might be a lesbian I panicked because I didn't want to wear that label. The word lesbian was loaded with outdated stereotypes and references that I felt didn't apply to me. When I came out my straight friends gave me the 'rubbish lesbian' moniker, probably because I didn't have a buzz cut, wear dungarees and hate men. It was a joke but it also revealed that the stereotype was very much alive and well.*

*Years on, and even though things have improved no end, outdated stereotypes like being cat-obsessed man haters in Birkenstocks still abound, if only as a source of comedy. This kind of stereotyping is a subtle but insidious undermining of self-esteem so I think even if it's meant in jest it should be tackled head on. We're all our own kind of lesbian.*

*Do people really think that who puts the spuds on defines your role as either man or woman? My straight friends' husbands do most of the cooking and my dad used to make a mean cheese on toast.*

## Lesbian Relationships: The Unwritten Roles.

A good relationship (a good lesbian relationship included) is like a bad Eddie Murphy movie – you get to play both the male and female roles.

Being in a lesbian relationship is like baking a cake and eating it too. I can have a hard day at the office AND get mad at myself when I haven't got dinner on the table when I get home.

So I find it strange, especially given the fact that my girlfriend and I are lesbians, that some people want to know who's 'the man', and who's 'the woman'. I thought the point was there was no man – not even figuratively.

They'll ask, "Who does the cooking?", which is really just their way of asking who wears the trousers. It's ridiculous. We both wear the trousers – and the skirts.

I don't like the idea of playing a role within a relationship and not being yourself. It doesn't sound like fun; unless of course one of you is a beautiful misunderstood bad girl in prison for a crime she didn't commit, and the other a lonely and confused prison governor who befriends her. Then it's okay.

When my girlfriend and I first got together we had the odd mix up over who was doing what. Things got done twice or not at all. When we packed to go on holiday, for example, it was a gamble as to whether we'd have what we needed the other side. It was double or nothing – I raise you two hairdryers, and I see you no hairbrush.

After a while some unwritten roles began to emerge. We didn't sit down and decide on who was doing what, we didn't even speak about it – it just happened. We just did what came naturally.

Now we've got our packaging routine down to a tee; I lay everything out on the bed, and my girlfriend squeezes everything in the case with great aplomb. It suits both our natural abilities: she has the mental agility and spatial awareness of a Krypton Factor contestant, and I enjoy laying out on the bed. She even does that rolling up your smalls and putting them inside shoes type of hardcore packing.

So that's how we role; sometimes I "cook", sometimes my girlfriend "cooks", and sometimes we like to eat out.

*I have 'butch' days and 'femme' days. As Donnie Osmond once sang, "I'm a little bit country. I'm a little bit rock n' roll". I think that on a scale of butch to femme I'm probably bang in the middle. But every now and then I have days where I feel I could wrestle an Action Man and come out on top.*

## Rocking the Bandana, or I Get My Butch On.

I want to wrestle a bear.

It's a school night, I've got friends arriving shortly for dinner, but I've got an urge to grapple a grizzly. There's only one explanation: I'm wearing a bandana.

It's amazing how the addition of some hanky head furniture can make you feel all sorts of badass. I'm loving it. I'm going to change my name to Snake and get an eye patch. Ooh! and some flaming tattoos.

It's impossible to apply eyeliner in the normal fashion while you're wearing a bandana. I have a deep urge to smudge a little under each eye – Rambo style. If I wasn't cooking for my friends I'd venture into war-torn Burma and rescue a group of Christian aid workers, but these pork chops won't cook themselves.

I'm also walking like I've got a space hopper wedged between my legs. I've stolen Cher Lloyd's swagger, and I'm so badass I'm not even going to return it; even if she asks nicely.

The virtues of bandana wearing are something of a revelation. There's only one negative so far; you can't drink gin and tonic whilst wearing a bandana. Can't be done. Oh well, I'll just have to crack open a beer instead – with my teeth.

The doorbell rings, but because I'm wearing my bandana I don't rush. I strut to the door, and fill the entrance with my body; one hand on the frame, the other on my hip. I'm oozing confidence.

My friend thrusts a poinsettia at me, clocks the bandana, and says, "Why are you dressed like a sushi chef?".

I visibly deflate. She's taken the wind right out of my hanky.

I avoided bandanas for years for fear they'd make me look like a great big lesbian. Now it turns out I needn't have bothered. Apparently, I'm a great big lesbian who looks like a sushi chef, in a bandana.

I've made the classic bandana-virgin error and tied it too thin. I need more girth. To rock the bandana you need to go big, like Axl Rose. I've managed to give mine the appearance of something issued by health and safety. Women won't be throwing their underwear at me; just the odd order of sashimi, if I'm lucky.

I slip if off. I'll pop it back on when she's gone. And somewhere in North London a bear heaves a sigh of relief.

*My friend called me a lipstick lesbian the other day and it was meant as a compliment. But I associate the term with girls who are trying being a lesbian on for a night. I think it's funny that people think they can determine whether you're butch or femme by whether you're sporting a thin smearing of lippy or not. There's a bit more to it than that.*

## I'm Officially a Red-Lipstick Lesbian.

Filled with festive spirit (sherry) I decided to give my mum an early Christmas present; I bought a red lipstick – for myself. She was over the moon. It was exactly what she'd always wanted. She turned to me, eyes welling with tears, and said, "you look so feminine". It's official. I am a lipstick lesbian.

Before we went our separate ways my mum whispered the secret to good red lips. She told me that it must never be undertaken lightly, or applied casually, in the back of a cab. "Always keep it in the lines, and go light on the eyes or you'll look like Coco the Clown, not Coco Chanel". Mental note: less honk honk, and more "ahahaha".

I've never really got my head, or indeed my lips, around lipstick. Its wonders are all too fleeting for my taste; no sooner have you put it on than it's come off again. Capturing the one moment when you are not either applying or reapplying lipstick would require Frozen Planet-esque time lapse photography. I'm more of an eyeliner kind of gal. For me the eyes definitely have it.

That said, I'm already loving this red lipstick. It's a whole different additive. This stuff stays on, and on, and on. You actually need to get a lip graft to remove it.

Feeling good about my bright red lips I arrange to meet a couple of my lesbian friends for drinks. As soon as they see the lips the ridicule begins. "You're a lesbian", they say, "you don't have to conform. You don't have to wear make up." But I like wearing make-up. It makes me feel good, and besides, without it I look like the photo on my driving licence.

Many of my lesbian friends don't see the point of lipstick. In their opinion wearing no make-up is far more empowering.

I'm beginning to feel like an outcast. I'm different from all the other lesbians. I've always thought of a killer red lipstick as being kick ass in a powerful female way. I imagine the genesis of red lipstick; melting Madonna's Blonde Ambition tour into a vat of pre-mixed Marilyn and a pinch of Geri Halliwell in a Union Jack dress. It's like liquid red kryptonite.

The bar woman arrives and asks what I'd like to drink. My thirsty friends are gobsmacked; they'd been jostling for attention for the best part of 15 minutes and been ignored. My light-up red lips have attracted her attention, and now we have alcohol in hand. Now that's what I call lip service.

*All I can say about this one is that you know it's true ladies. IKEA is our spiritual Mecca. Lesbians are drawn to IKEA like moths to an IKEA UPLID outside light. What are you doing this weekend? Fancy grabbing a coffee and coming to IKEA for some tea lights? I'll let you get meatballs...*

## IKEA – A Little Trip Into Bank Holiday Hell Anyone?

The sun that shone all week has vanished behind the clouds. There are no fans or hot dog rolls to be found within a 60-mile radius. The words, '2 cocktails for £8.50' have been scrawled on an A-board outside my local. This can only mean one thing: August bank holiday.

A bank holiday is a terrifying prospect because it usually heralds at least one trip to that aircraft hanger of corrugated hell: IKEA. I've been known to spend my entire bank holiday lost in their labyrinthine layout, wandering disorientated, and clutching a bag of coloured tea lights that I've convinced myself we need.

My girlfriend will say, "Let's go to IKEA" in such sweet, dulcet tones, but it's laden with menace. This is where lesbian relationships go to die. Every one of IKEA's mouth-blown vases is filled with the soul of a lesbian relationship that didn't survive a difference of opinion over napkins. They can't escape, because the neck is barely wide enough to hold a single stem, so they're forced to remain inside quasi-ornaments for eternity.

Why do we do it to ourselves? Why would we leave the quiet street where we live and the promise of a cold pint at the local pub, to drive to a retail park with every other lesbian couple in Britain? Once there, we'll be forced to creep slowly past the one soon-to-be-free parking space a hundred times, getting ready to nab it when the engine starts up like a four-wheeled game of musical chairs. Meanwhile the couple occupying the space are busy loading an entire kitchen into their MINI Clubman.

If we do survive the journey and find a parking space, then IKEA will try to divide us with 'stuff'. Nothing will have you running for the exit faster than seeing the woman you love holding up a turquoise fish-shaped, ice-cube tray and giving you her 'come to buy' eyes. Few relationships are strong enough to withstand an onslaught of (A) tiny Tupperware nests, (B) cutlery that has clear blue handles and bubbles inside it, and (C) a big red plastic jug that might be "fun for summer".

My girlfriend's IKEA storage fetish has become my own nemesis. She will go there simply to buy things to put other things in. I don't get it. Her idea of heaven is pants wrapped inside a hand woven KOMPLEMENT compartment, inside an underwear drawer, inside a chest of drawers. It's an enigma. So I know there will come a time when I will want to end it right there in the home office section –usually as we are considering six more transparent boxes with lids. But then I'll remember and say, "NO. This is what IKEA wants. They want us to throw away nine years of happy memories on a polypropylene plastic box that will fit under the bed and house our carpet off-cuts. We can't let them beat us!".

Then I will grab my girlfriend, shake her by shoulders and beseech her, "For the love of God woman let's just go and get some meatballs."

*Another brilliant lesbian stereotype is the sporty lez. I am about as un-sporty as it gets. Having said that, I do like to watch.*

## I'm Very Sporty: I Love to Watch.

I think I've caught Olympic fever. My speech is peppered with involuntarily shouts of, "Gold!" as if I'm suffering from a rare form of Spandau Ballet Tourette's. Yesterday, I became emotional at the sight of Daley Thompson in a white shell suit, jogging with a flaming torch. I fear I may never tire of hearing what Michael Phelps had for lunch.

The last time I was this excited about coloured rings, Fox's had just reinstated their purple and yellow biscuit. The games haven't even started, and already I can't get enough. Even the ever-present sight of Usain Bolt's Lycra-encased moose knuckle, in full HD, has done very little to dampen my ardour.

My enthusiasm for the Olympics has come as a shock to people, because I don't 'do' sport myself. When God was handing out sporting prowess most of my lesbian friends were all at the front of the queue, and I was right at the back. I only joined the queue because I mistook it for an All Saints sample sale.

I'm very clumsy, so if I'd had a sporty bone in my body I'd have broken it by now, along with the arm I broke somersaulting (on a bouncy castle), the elbow I broke roller blading (in the drive) and the wrist I broke falling over a tennis racket I left in the hall.

My dad on the other hand is super-competitive. He has the sport gene for sure, but he just refused to pass it to me. I was his doubles tennis partner for a while, and he never let me take a shot. The ball would be falling on my racket, and he'd shove me out the way and yell, "Mine!" It was like playing with a toddler.

People think that lesbians and sport go together, like cat videos and YouTube. They'll ask, "What sports do you play?" as if it's a given. They're shocked when I tell them that I can't even 'bat for the other side'. At school I was the last one to be picked when the rounders team was chosen, and I've still never made it to fourth base. The only thing I ever scored on the playing field at school was a bottle of White Lightning.

I'm rubbish at sport – and I'm fine with that. Give me a comfy armchair over a chafed nipple any day. Had my audition for The Spice Girls been successful my moniker would have been Spectator Spice. Instead of the famous high-kick, my signature move would have involved throwing myself down on the sofa and crossing my feet in front of the telly. Zig-a-zig-ah!

I've even managed to lay my hands, very respectfully, on a couple of women's beach volleyball tickets. My dad, on the other hand, is going to watch Swedish men play handball. I think we both know who's the real winner here.

*At first I was absolutely adamant we would never get a cat. I saw the addition of a cat as surrendering to the lesbian stereotype. Just as I never imagined myself as a lesbian I had never pictured myself as a cat lady. How things change!*

## Crazy Cat Ladies Host a Lip Service Dinner Party.

My girlfriend and I don't have an elephant in the room, but we do have a six-foot-high cat tree we can no longer ignore. The Squeeze wrote a song about the lesbian friends we're having over for dinner and an episode of everyone's fave TV show Lip Service – they're too 'cool for cats'. They'll take one look at the Feline Fun Park in our living room, and we'll be consigned to the crazy cat women pile forever.

Every inch of the house is covered cat stuff; it looks like Pets At Home has thrown up in there. It's all got to go, every sparkly, jangly, feathery, squeaky, sisal-y bit of it. The cats have disdained every gift I've ever given them, but my little clear-out has suddenly piqued their interest. I remind them what curiosity did and they take their leave of the situation.

Our guests arrive and there's no sign of the cats or their paraphernalia. But as soon as the starters are over I hear a distinctive, tap, tap, tap. It's a cat dragging something down the stairs. The question is what? I've hidden all the cat toys so what in God's name can she be dragging? Then I see a flash of crumpled silk in her mouth and I know that she's about to drop a large pair of pants at my guest's feet. My pants. It's a passive aggressive masterclass.

I screech my chair back, scoop her up, remove my pants and put her back down. No one saw the pants, but it was a clear declaration of war – revenge for the removal of the cat tree. This cat is a loose cannon, and I fear she's only just getting started.

"What's your cat's name?" asks one of our guests, "No! Let me guess. Emily Dickinson? That's the sort of name lesbians usually give cats."

Oh God. Her name. I'd completely forgotten her name. The minute I reveal it I'm done for, because they'll never believe that her name came first. They'll think I named my cat after a famous crush. I'll have to lie. Make up a name. Quick, think of some names.

The cat seizes this lull in proceedings to strike again. I hadn't planned on having entertainment between courses, but perhaps I should have booked a belly dancer, or arranged for some synchronised swimmers to pop by. It might have saved us all from the performance my cat is now giving us. She's mounted her female companion, and is pinning her to the ground and aggressively licking her ears.

I shout at her hoping to get her to dismount and go back to whatever godforsaken embroidered cat bed she came from, "LEXY! NO!"

"Ahh. Sexy Lexy. Of course. You would name your cat after your favourite Lip Service character – that makes sense." Our guests are vindicated.

The sound of raucous laughter and ridicule reverberates around the kitchen. But then a hush descends over our little dinner party, as if the sight of Lexy forcing her way into another's affections so brazenly has stirred up an ancient hurt. Finally, someone says what we've all been thinking: "Poor Cat."

*When God was handing out practical life skills such as map reading or DIY to all the lesbians I know, I must have been in the toilet, probably struggling to flush the cistern and hoping that another, more practical lesbian would arrive and rescue me.*

## Directionally Challenged: If in Doubt, Keep Going Straight.

I'm so crap at directions I sometimes wonder if I'd ever have discovered my sexual orientation had it not been for GPS. I would have probably missed the turning and just continued going straight.

People wrongly assume that because I'm a lesbian I'll be good at practical things like woodwork or directions, as if lesbians have natural navigational skills. If that's true, I've never found them. The fact that I found my way out of the closet at all is nothing short of a miracle.

When other people get lost, they stumble upon picturesque ancient ruins or a little off-the-beaten-track pub. My kind of lost involves driving in ever-decreasing circles around a one-way system screaming at the sat nav woman until, exhausted, I pull over and call my girlfriend to guide me in.

This weekend we were enjoying a leisurely lunch in Brussels when my girlfriend suddenly leapt to her feet and announced that our train was leaving in 20 minutes. For some reason she thought that I had my eye on the time, when in fact I had my eye on the Tiramisu.

In the frenzy that followed, she ordered me to run ahead, find the Eurostar, and begin check-in, while she retrieved our bag from left luggage. Find Eurostar? Was she crazy? I can't even find the North Star.

I spent the next 10 minutes ricocheting around the terminal like a projectile pinball unable to find the check-in desk. Aware that time was ticking away, despair set in: My girlfriend will kill me; I'm going to go round and round this frites kiosk for eternity; I may never get to watch Tulisa's 'Judges Houses'.

By the time I found check-in I didn't know whether I was coming or going. I was sweaty, I was tearful, and I was without hope. I was also without a ticket as it turned out, because my girlfriend had kept mine so that I wouldn't lose it.

One tannoy announcement later and we're reunited only to find that our train doesn't actually leave for another hour. I feel somewhat vindicated. I might have been lost, but this time it was my girlfriend's timekeeping that was found wanting.

PART SEVEN

# SHIT PEOPLE SAY

## Including What a Waste, I Wish I Was a Lesbian and Who's the Man?

*The funny things that people have said to me on finding out that I'm a lesbian have always been a rich vein of content for my columns. When I first started writing the column I collected them. I'd jot them down in a notebook or make a mental note. Often I was too shocked, or unsure how to respond at the time, and it was only with hindsight that I understood the social dynamics and the full implication of what people meant.*

*Some people seem to think that just by telling them, total strangers, that you're gay you're somehow asking for their approval. Others try to be über PC and will bore you with stories of the one other lesbian they met once. They'll test your lesbian trivia as if they believe your brain will have automatic recall of the number of times Martina won Wimbledon. The following columns grew out of those kinds of encounters.*

*I've noticed that some people feel obliged to seem really chuffed when they hear you're a lesbian. The more confident I became about my sexuality the more irritating this unprompted quasi-approval became.*

## "You're a lesbian. Great! We're totally fine with that."

If there is one thing that's worse than telling people that I'm lesbian, it's listening to them tell me how 'okay' they are with it.

From time to time I have to reveal my sexuality as necessary context for a story. I'm not making a statement, I'm not seeking approval, I'm explaining why having two blokes from the Council in your bedroom at 2am, with noise monitoring equipment, isn't ideal.

I don't want to make a drama out of it, because to me it's just a fact of life – like cellulite. Not so for many of the people I tell. They feel compelled to either offer me useless platitudes like, "you can't help who you fall in love with", or let me how REALLY okay they are with it. No. Really.

"Congratulations!" people say, as if I've announced I've won the gene pool lotto. It's difficult to know how to respond to such expressions of joy at my sapphic status except to say, "Thanks, I guess I just got lucky."

Some greet the news with a level of enthusiasm usually reserved for the words "Free Bar". They just keep repeating "GREAT. That's really GREAT." Great is deployed immediately on hearing the word lesbian. It's like a conversational airbag – designed to protect them from the full impact of what you are saying.

"It doesn't bother us" or "We're fine with it" is usually the precursor to a very dull story involving another lesbian they've met. “We had an accountant once who was a lesbian. She was very nice.” The connection is always as tenuous as a mobile signal outside the M25.

A girl I told this week responded by saying, “I wish I’d done that before I got married.” I think she was confusing being a lesbian with taking a gap year. Either that or she had forgotten to add ‘lesbianism’ to her wedding planning checklist – it usually follows ‘book hen night in Magaluf’.

I prefer it when people just act normally and don’t feel the need to talk to me about ‘lesbian things’, or impress me with their bank of lesbian trivia.

For the record: Martina Navratilova was the best-ever Wimbledon champion, I agree. Yes, Ellen DeGeneres is very funny, and Jonathon Ross’s daughter is also a lesbian. And before you ask – I don’t know any of them.

*Ugh, I hate this sort of backhanded compliment. The implication is that people think it's much easier to be in a relationship without men. What rubbish! Relationships are hard no matter who they are with and thinking otherwise trivialises lesbians. (Climbs down off soap box.)*

## "I wish I was a lesbian."

I've just come out to a colleague over a glass of wine and some antipasti. She took it very well, in fact she starred whimsically into her wine glass and said, "I wish I was a lesbian." What does she think I am, a genie's lamp? I'd better set her straight before she tries to give me a rub.

Being a lesbian is a funny thing to wish for. A big lottery win, a different ending to Homeland, Dannii Minogue back on X-Factor, or Big Macs that actually burn calories, those are the kinds of things you'd wish for if you had the chance, surely? Oh, and world peace of course. *Miss World face*

Straight women have said they wish they were a lesbian to me a number of times and every time I hear it I think the same thing: "Do you though? Do you really? Or are you just mad at your boyfriend for mistakenly peeing in your handbag again when drunk?"

I think they believe that being a lesbian is somehow easier because there's no man involved. But being in a relationship with blokes is a cinch in comparison because they don't have a clue what you're thinking. They ask if you're alright, and if you say yes that's good enough for them, they're off down the pub. Anyone who's ever tried to answer their lesbian partner's, "What's wrong?", with, "nothing" would know that the following 24 hours make Jack Bauer's interrogation scenes look like that Haribo advert where the dad's eaten all the fried eggs.

It trivialises lesbian relationships to suggest that they're somehow devoid of the everyday drama and the emotional roller coaster that is part of any functioning relationship. Do they think lesbian couples never fight over the stray pants on the bathroom floor or who last emptied the dishwasher? It's not all shared wardrobes, running each other baths, and listening to each other's problems over cups of herbal tea. Being a lesbian isn't just one big platonic sleepover. This shit is real. It's a lot of fun, granted, but it's still real.

The funny thing is I used to wish I was straight like my friends, but now I'm glad I'm a lesbian. I love my life and wouldn't wish it any other way. There are still times, however, when I wish that being a lesbian was as effortless as being straight. I wish that showing affection in public didn't feel like making a statement and was just a simple invisible gesture the way it is for my sister and her husband. I'm sure if my colleague had a taster of what it's like to be treated the way many lesbians are she'd be more careful what she wished for.

So back at the bar I decide I'm going to set her straight, "Why do you wish you were a lesbian?" Maybe it's the wine talking, but rather less eruditely than I was expecting she says, "Because I think lesbians are cool."

This woman clearly knows what she's talking about. Who am I to argue with her?

*This happened as my ex and I wandered around Soho on a balmy Summer evening. We were just waxing lyrical about how lucky we were to live in such a tolerant and diverse city when some bloke staggered out of a pub, looked us up and down and said with a tut, "What a waste." It wasn't as if he even said it to upset us– it was just his unchecked thought process leaking out as commentary. What do they think is wasted exactly? I think now if someone shouted this I'd stop and ask because I'm genuinely curious but at this point I didn't have the balls – oh wait, maybe that's what he meant?*

## "What a waste!"

I don't understand why anyone would think that my being a lesbian is somehow a 'waste', like throwing away perfectly good fruit. I've always found it quite a creative use of my natural resources.

Last week my girlfriend and I were enjoying a late night hand-in-hand stroll through Soho, when a passing bloke shouted, "What a waste!" at us. Had we walked all the way back to the 1900s? Whatever happened to cat calling?

I turned around to see the culprit staring at me, tutting like my mum used to when I left my broccoli untouched. I half expected him to follow up with, "there are sex starved men in the world, you know!".

How could a man with no obvious natural ability accuse me of somehow squandering my talent? It's not like I gave up a promising career in heterosexuality; I was never that successful at it.

At least we had something in common; I wanted to set him straight too. Boy, when I was done with him his days of abusing random strangers would be well and truly over. In the end, however, I settled for a cold, hard stare and an epic flounce off.

I think he got the message.

I'm told that people mean such things as a compliment. The implication being: I *could* get a man if I wanted. I could also get a degree in Parapsychology from Coventry University, but I don't want to be a clairvoyant – or do I?

I have a sneaking suspicion that it might be the waste of space that troubles people. They imagine my vagina standing empty and disused like a rundown fairground ride. But it's not a condemned mineshaft. There's no Keep Out sign hanging at the entrance.

What some people fail to understand is that being a lesbian is about *so* much more than sex. It's about helping your girlfriend pick through a rubbish sack looking for an earring that she's not entirely sure she even dropped in there. It's about accompanying her to IKEA on bank holiday Monday to buy a bracket for the broken kitchen cabinet, only to be told it's been discontinued. These are the sort of useless pursuits that are still worthwhile when you find someone you love spending time with.

I can't speak for my girlfriend, of course, but I'm sure I'm not *entirely* wasted on her.

*If like me you have a great set of straight friends and then you suddenly launch yourself into the gay scene and meet like-minded lesbians it can be a bit threatening for them. I think they fear that you've got more in common and they're losing you to a bunch of lesbians.*

## "You've gone a bit too gay."

I'm browsing Selfridges ground floor and regaling a straight friend with an anecdote from last night, when she says, all matter-of-fact, "You've gone too gay." I knew I shouldn't have worn the rainbow caftan.

This statement just came out of the blue. It was like the verbal equivalent of being spritzed by an overzealous perfume salesperson. I'm a bit taken aback. Can you actually be 'too gay'? I thought 'gay' was like hats, shoes or bags, and you could never have too much of a good thing, but apparently it's more like Botox.

"You never used to be this gay." She's making me sound like a faulty product she's trying to return. I'm not a big fan of labels, but last time I checked, mine clearly said gay, right next to Made in Torquay. Perhaps I'll be part of a nationwide recall, like a tin of tainted tuna, and she'll get her money back.

I get the feeling we're about to workshop this to death right here, and I don't want my life on display with all the other miscellany – someone might buy it. I try ushering her in the direction of confectionery to sweeten her up, but she's having none of it. "You're always with les-bi-ans these days" she says, deliberately dragging out the syllables of the word to make them sound boring. I notice the woman behind the counter has smokey eyes on sticks, so it can't be that dull.

It's true I do have a number of lesbian friends. But I don't pick my friends on the basis of their sexuality. I tell her that to me friendship is about sharing the same world view and values, not to mention the same sense of humour. It's also a question of lifestyle. Unlike many of my straight friends, this one included, the lesbians I know don't have kids, so we've naturally gravitated towards each other – like planets – minus the big bang.

Finally she confesses, "I'm afraid you'll just lose interest in your straight friends." Now I get it. She's concerned that we'll grow apart, and I'll turn entirely to the dark side. She needn't worry. I'm not about to ditch my straight family altogether, and head off to some sort of Lesbian Death Star. I've got no plans to move to Stoke Newington.

Thankfully she seems reassured and we move onto more important things – like lunch. "What do you talk about with these les-bi-an friends anyway?" she asks, adding with a burdened sigh, "slip-ons?". At first I think she's making a 'comfortable shoe' joke, but then it clicks, "Do you mean strap-ons?". She laughs so much she sprays me with salt beef. Now that's what I call a Hallmark moment.

*This next one is a variation on "Who wears the trousers? Who does the cooking?" I think I've probably made this point a few times in a few different columns, but it's something that crops up time and again.*

## "But dude, who's the groom?"

At the wonderful, and very civil-partnership of my dear friends this week someone revealed that a lesbian friend of hers who was recently married was asked "Which one of you is the groom?" Really? A frantic last minute squirt of dry shampoo, or a little dab of glue on a false eyelash – that's the closest you get to a groom at a lesbian wedding.

People love to ask questions like this because they like to assign traditional roles, particularly when it comes to weddings. They want to know who's going to be wearing the dress and who the trousers – literally and metaphorically. It's as if the idea of a wedding proceeding without a groom would rip asunder the natural order of things and chaos would somehow reign: the moon will turn red, summer will follow winter, and rabbits will start eating foxes.

I remember one older relative's baffled response to me coming out: "But...who'll do the cooking?" As if the dynamics of a healthy relationship can be distilled down into who whips up an omelette of an evening. Is it really that simple? She clearly thought that as two women we'd argue over who did the cooking. There'd be carnage in the kitchen. We'd start squaring up to each other with mezzalunas, vying for control of the cutting boards.

It's amazing that people still think this way. Do they really think the first thing you do upon entering a lesbian relationship is flip a coin, or each other, to see who'll be the guy and who'll be the girl. Madness. I prefer to look at relationships as being made up of two people with complementary life skills. There are those that read the maps and those that can drive the cars. Those that can see painting a room through to completion, and those who are a crying wreck after one wall. Some people cook, and others can remove a trapped 30 Rock DVD wihout electrocuting themselves. It's less of a gender thing and more of a survival thing. It's nature's way of keeping the population alive.

So next time I get asked, "Who does the cooking?" I won't cringe away, or try to make them feel better about asking such an inane question. Instead I'll face it head on. Look them in the eyes and say "We're lesbians. We both cook. But we prefer to eat out".

*A few years ago we had a guest to stay who was divorced and a serial dater of men. She kept making reference to our wonderful 'lifestyle' as if all lesbians lived the same 'lifestyle'.*

## "It's a wonderful lesbian lifestyle."

We've just had a visit from The Homo Inspector. She was no Alex Polizzi, but I'm pleased to say that she gave our 'lesbian lifestyle' her highly commended Four Star seal of approval. I'm just wondering where to stick the rosette.

The woman in question was a friend of my girlfriend. Recently divorced from her husband she came to stay with us for a change of scene and a quiet break from her three kids for a few days.

She entered the house, put her bags down, and announced "Welcome to the lesbian lifestyle!".

Uh oh! There's been a misunderstanding. She thinks she's booked a 'lesbian lifestyle', and all we had available is a plain ole lifestyle. This has happened to us before. People think they're getting late nights and clubbing, and when they find out it's Frozen Planet and fajitas they demand a refund.

I needn't have worried in this case, because she was full of praise. Everything from our light and airy low-key lesbian décor, to our locally sourced ethically produced lesbian bacon met with her approval. We couldn't make tea, eat an olive, or read a paper without her crediting its success entirely to our 'lesbian lifestyle'.

A simple morning coffee prompted her to well up "Wow. Fresh coffee. I could totally get used to this lesbian lifestyle!" I tried to explain that fresh coffee is not technically part of the lifestyle, it comes as standard. She wouldn't have it; apparently, the men she's dated don't place the same emphasis on a freshly cracked bean in the morning, which is a shame really.

Dinner that night and once again she was effusive. “You are so lucky to be able to eat sushi together.” In her experience men don’t consider sushi to be a meal, so she never gets to indulge (yes, there may be a subtext here). I tried to suggest it might just be down to personal taste, but she was adamant that sushi à deux was most definitely another privilege of the ‘lesbian lifestyle’.

When it came time for checking out, she insisted on a group hug and one final pep talk before she left. “I’m so proud of you. You guys have really created a great lifestyle for yourselves.” And with that she assured us that she would definitely be recommending the ‘lesbian lifestyle’ to all her friends.

*This column is a combination of a few things that I've heard said, in jest of course, but which only serves to support dated stereotypes. "I'd make a good lesbian, I've got two cats", or "I'd be a good lesbian, I'm vegetarian." You'd only make a good lesbian if you like to sleep with women – if not, chances are you wouldn't.*

## "I'd make a good lesbian."

Out of the blue, over a cheese board, a straight friend of mine suddenly announces, "I'd make a good lesbian." It's easy for her to say, even with a mouthful of Brie, but I think she's forgotten an important pre-requisite: women. She's never been sexually or romantically attracted to women.

I wonder what's prompted this little declaration? This friend spends a lot of time in our company, but you don't become a good lesbian by osmosis. I only hope it's got nothing to do with Angelina Jolie. If I had a penny for every straight girl who's confessed they 'would' with Angelina, well I'd probably have copper poisoning. Wanting sexy time with Angelina doesn't make you a lesbian. It just proves you have a pulse.

I fear she may be about to launch Julie Andrews-style into a list of some of her favourite (stereotypically lesbian) things: cats, quiche and quinoa. But liking the same things that lesbians supposedly like doesn't mean you'd make a good lesbian, it just means you have good taste.

As if reading my mind, she clarifies that she'd make a good lesbian because she's located her stopcock. I'm a lesbian and I couldn't tell you what a stopcock was, let alone where to find it. It sounds like a souped-up version of a chastity belt or a nickname for Spanx. Being handy about the house doesn't make you a good lesbian. It just means you're the one digging around under the stairs for a masonry nail, while your partner's watching Come Dine with Me.

She then begins a five-minute diatribe about how men are to blame for everything from war and road rage, to the invention of the Kit Kat Chunky, the need for pedestal mats, and the re-commissioning of Top Gear. Her conclusion: "We'd be better off without them." It's compelling stuff and eruditely argued after a few glasses of wine, but lesbians aren't seeking the complete eradication of the male species. We just don't want to make the two-backed beast with them.

"Lesbians are proof that women can survive without men financially and emotionally. Think about it. It's the ultimate independent lifestyle." says my friend. She concludes that on that basis there should be a little lesbian in all women. It's such an impassioned speech that I decide to make her an honorary lesbian.

She raises her glass. "To the lesbian inside all of us." Hear, hear.

*The following scenario has happened to me a couple of times at parties and I'm intrigued by some people's reaction to the news I'm a lesbian. I think it's common that they panic and want you to know they're totally okay with it. They frantically scrabble around for any other lesbian they can tell you about in an attempt to underline that they're cool with it. Trouble is, it's not really that interesting.*

## "I know another lesbian, not very well."

"Melinda? Was that her name?" I'm waiting for a woman I've just been introduced to to remember the name of the one other lesbian she knows – evidently not all that well. It seems like every straight person I meet wants to tell me about the other lesbian they've met before. At least they think she was a lesbian. I'm not sure why people do this but they do. Perhaps it's to reassure me that they're really fine with the fact I'm a lesbian. No, *really* fine with it. Couldn't be *more* fine with it.

Like all lesbians remembered vaguely the lesbian she's thinking of is very nice, from memory. If she could only remember her name! "Melissa?" Sadly, no. So, I wait, while all the mini quiches are plucked from the buffet behind me, and I wait, stuck there, like this name is stuck, probably under a pile of T'Pau lyrics in my new acquaintance's brain. Finally: "Melanie!" The husband, who has kept schtum till now, suddenly animates. "She was a lesbian?" His wife responds with a solemn nod that at once confirms this sad news, and reveals that she's not all that fine with it after all.

Sometimes people ask if I know the lesbian in question – the one they barely know themselves – because all lesbians know each other right? There was the estate agent who dropped a steady stream of made-up-sounding lesbian couples into all our conversations. I'd complain about kitchen cabinet capacity and she'd counter "Debbie and Emma had a shaker kitchen put in – great depth – do you know them?". And though I never once admitted to knowing any of these local flipping house lesbians, she kept a steady stream of them coming. "Have you seen Kim and Julie's side return?" All the time I'd be thinking "Lady, I have no idea who you are talking about, and I've never seen their extension." But invariably I'd just settle for "No, but it sounds good."

"I think you'd really like Melanie," the lady at the party is now saying to me, the person she met five minutes ago about this other lesbian that she sort of knows vaguely. I'd like to call her on it and say "Really, on what possible basis?" But instead I find myself cooing "She sounds nice." This is a lie. Because I don't know anything about her and because they clearly don't know anything about her either. Except her name which does sound nice, and oh that she's a lesbian. At least they're pretty sure she's a lesbian.

She seems so genuinely excited by the prospect of Melissa and I (was that her name?) getting to know each other better – better than she knows either of us at any rate – that I feel obliged to feign interest, "What's she like?" "She's…." I can see her desperately feeling around for a suitable generic adjective with which to describe this memorable lesbian she once met. "She's lovely…" If that adjective were any woolier it would have pom-poms on it. Then I see a glint in her eye that tells me she's landed on the perfect description of Miranda – one that's really going seal the deal. Satisfied, she says, "She's a bit like Clare Balding." If I had a pound for every time someone has described their lesbian friend who I absolutely must meet as, "a bit like Clare Balding" I'd be a very rich lesbian, who some might describe as a bit like Clare Balding. But to bring this to her attention now would be bad etiquette, so instead I intone dutifully, "I love Clare Balding," because I do. To which my new friend responds, "Ooh so do I!" I can hardly believe how much we've all got in common.

*I've saved the worst till last. It shows terrible self-awareness for someone to openly put down lesbians in front of someone they know is a lesbian. To add insult to injury, they give you what they believe to be a compliment by saying "but that's not you darling, you're not like that." Meaning you're not a real lesbian. Blerg, as Tina Fey would say.*

## "But you're not one of those lesbians!"

From time to time people apparently forget that I'm a lesbian and make jokes about other lesbians in front of me. Funnily enough this memory lapse on their part usually coincides with me remembering why I never really liked them in the first place.

When I challenge people about these 'jokes' their stock response is usually "Oh, but we're not talking about you. You're not like that." As if that makes it okay. People have no idea how insulting they are being; far from it, they actually think they're paying me a compliment. What am I supposed to say? "Thanks, you're quite funny for a bigot."

I sometimes think it's a case of The Lesbians are All Right just as long as you know them. Take last week, for example. A bloke I work with is in the middle of subjecting me to a hilarious impression of a 'dyke' who used to be his boss. He's clearly forgotten that I'm a lesbian. This isn't going to end well.

His impression consists of him repeating, "Hello. I'm a lesbian," in a lower register than his voice. It's not going to win him a slot at the Royal Variety. Frankly it's far too predictable and there's not enough satire. It's just another lame example of a white man impersonating lesbians; at least this one hasn't got his own blog – at least I hope not. I try clearing my throat to make him stop and consider what he's saying. "Ahem". But the penny doesn't drop. "Are you okay?" he says, "Do you need water?" Water? No

I don't need water. What I need is for you to get your head out of your arse and realise that you're being offensive.

"Bloody lesbians! They're so demanding" he continues oblivious. He has NO idea. This woman doesn't sound like she was being demanding. She was just doing her job well. If he thinks lesbians are demanding he should try sleeping with one. Actually, something tells me he might have tried sleeping with one thus the 'sour grapes' impression.

The time for subtle warnings is over. I'm going to have to spell it out for him. "Er. Hello. Les-bi-an," I say gesticulating wildly at myself. At this point, completely unabashed, he smiles and says "But you're not one of *those* lesbians."

I'm definitely the sleeping with women kind. What other kind is there?

PART EIGHT

# LESBIAN FAILS

## The Nail Fail, Sapphic Seductions on The High Street and an Inappropriate Kiss.

*On the face of it, being a lesbian seems an impossible thing to fail at, but I often felt that I'd failed. Failure means many things: failure to come out, failure to come out in a way that didn't embarrass the hell out of people, myself included, failure to read situations and, more often than not, my own internal insecurities about my sexuality manifested themselves in general awkwardness.*

*It's really this awkwardness that I wanted to capture, because day to day that's what we face, particularly as newly-out lesbians, when the world is set up for straight people and they're programmed to make certain assumptions.*

*Since writing the column below I've actually moved into a flat next door to my therapist! She's no longer my therapist, now she's my cat sitter and plant waterer.*

## Not Stalking But (Flat) Hunting.

I'm in the middle of a misunderstanding of Miranda-worthy proportions. I set out this morning to meet an estate agent to view a property that I knew was in the general vicinity of my therapist's flat. I hadn't realised quite how close it was, however, because it turns out it's not just down the street, or even further down the row, it's bang on her doorstep. I hadn't planned to nuzzle doormats with her, but I really need a flat and in this part of North London a good one bedroom is harder to find than a decent therapist.

I decided not to mention that I was planning to view a flat nearby at our last session because why create drama, when I might not even like the flat? But I do like the flat. In fact I'm just about to sign on the dotted line when she pops her head around the door to talk to the agent and spots me. I can only imagine how this looks.

Her face seems to be registering surprise and terror at the same time. She probably thinks I'm secretly in love with her and I'm moving in downstairs so I can live out my secret sexual fantasies and pretend that we live together in one big house flat. I am that lesbian stalker. God I hope she doesn't think that. She must know that's not in my nature? I'm an avoider, not a stalker.

I want to reassure her that it's not what it looks like. There's a perfectly reasonable explanation for why we're standing just a few metres from her consulting room. But instead I gesture a silent acknowledgement. I raise my hand but don't actually follow through with the wave, so my now raised hand is just hanging in the air like an admission of guilt. Less of a "hello" and more "Fair cop. You caught me."

I don't even think I'm supposed to say "Hello", am I? Unless I've misunderstood, the first rule of therapy is don't contact your therapist out of your allocated hour. The second rule of therapy is don't contact your therapist out of your allocated hour. The third rule of therapy is – and I'm guessing here – don't curb crawl or move in next door to your therapist.

I start to say something when the agent interrupts me, "Sarah this is your new neighbour." Then she turns to my therapist and says, "Great news! Sarah's going to be moving in next week. I'm sure you two will get on well." My therapist says nothing but manages to produce a sort of smile. She walks to the door, turns to give me 'the look', and then she's gone. I'm guessing we'll be talking about this on Monday.

*Still clenching my butt and cringing about this one. We never did do that return dinner.*

## An Inappropriate Kiss: A Warm Welcome Gets Out Of Hand.

I've just accidentally kissed my friend's new girlfriend on the lips. I was going for a warm welcome, but things have become a lot warmer than I'd anticipated.

I didn't mean to kiss her on the lips. I went to kiss her on the cheek, but I slipped on the hallway runner and the jolt altered my trajectory just enough that my closed lips briefly connected with hers. If it had ended there it would have been okay, but we both opened our mouths in surprise and there followed a sort of muffled kissing sound. I have effectively properly kissed her on the lips. Awkward.

Should I acknowledge it, laugh it off, or pretend it didn't happen? This is the reason I'm not a fan of the face kiss. It's unclear whether you should do one, or two, or in the case of the Swiss, three. There's too much room for error; too much risk of a head butt, a nose kiss or worse a total diss, where they go in for the third kiss and you've already gone.

This kind of inappropriate intimacy is best reserved for strangers, not people you are going to have to see again. I was on the bus once and it pulled away quickly causing me to stumble forward and place my hands on the window in front of me. What I hadn't noticed was that there was a woman between the window and me. I had my legs wide apart, my hands on the window either side of her head, and my breasts were now touching hers. We had full body contact; our 'areas' were actually touching until the bus came to a halt. When I finally regained my balance I didn't know whether to do a runner or get her number.

What if my friend's girlfriend now thinks I'm that predatory lesbian that she's read about in the Daily Mail? The end of the evening is looming and all I can think about is the goodbyes. I must not give her another inappropriate smacker lest she think the first time wasn't an accident. But if I don't acknowledge that she's leaving she might think I don't trust myself to get that close to her again. This is wretched.

When the moment of truth arrives, I'm so determined not to repeat the earlier mistake that instead of going for the kiss I opt for the hug. I suddenly and impulsively clasp her to my bosom as if she's a long lost friend. She immediately begins to draw away, but I'm still trying to pull off the goodbye hug. The whole thing has turned into a sort of terrible protracted headlock. We are left holding on to each other, like two exhausted boxers, neither wanting to break the clinch and face the inevitable embarrassing fallout. I finally let go the hug only to hear my girlfriend making plans for a re-match; dinner at their place next week. Oh God, this is only round one.

*Coming out in a very girly environment, to a lot of very girly girls all discussing their fellas while the manicurist is holding your hand is probably asking for a high degree of awkwardness.*

## Nail Fail: The Art Of Coming Out Over a Manicure.

Nearly every lesbian porn film I've ever seen has featured 'lesbians' with ridiculously long red fingernails. They're always bouncing around on a bed surrounded by dozens of dildos and slashing at each other like Freddie Krueger. These movies should be reclassified as horror.

The lesbians I know have well-trimmed nails, and personally speaking I love a manicure. Maybe it's got something to do with the word itself. Man-i-cure. It sounds like some sort of lesbian conversion camp.

The thing is, in all the years I've been going to the same nail salon, I've never actually come out to the girls who work there. It may be because they're straighter than a Brazilian blow dry. Call me old-fashioned, but I'm not comfortable telling a straight girl that I'm a lesbian while she's holding my hand in hers.

But because I haven't told them, they think I'm a total nail fail. They have no idea that growing my nails could mean enforced celibacy, they think it's about lack of effort. So every time I visit I have to go through the charade of promising to try and grow my nails next time. I really need to set them straight.

Today I arrive and join the long row of other clients sitting shoulder to shoulder and clucking away about man troubles like a load of battery beauty hens. The woman next to me is reading aloud from Grazia. I'm pretty sure the only DIVA she's ever heard of is Kim Kardashian.

The nail technician takes one look at my nails and says "Look at this! You promised you'd grow them. What are these?" Er, my hands? She holds up my neatly nipped nails, and all the other customers look at me as if to say, "Ah bless". I'm cut to the quick. I feel like I'm four years old and I've just crashed my parents' dinner party wearing my mum's heels.

"Don't you want nails like these?" She is gesturing at the impressively long and polished nails of the woman next to me. No actually. My girlfriend would need to fashion a falconry glove for her privates if I had those talons. She'd take one look at my Edward Scissorhands and close up like a clam.

"I bet your boyfriend would like it," she declares, playing to the crowd. I sense that she's not going to let me off this hook this time. I need to put an end to this charade once and for all. "Girlfriend" I correct her. The hens tense. There's an uncomfortable silence, except for the sound of Grazia pages gently flapping under the nail dryer.

"Er. What colour have you chosen?" She's pretending that nothing's happened. I pass her the bottle. "Ah", she says, swallowing hard. "Mink Muffs. Good choice."

*God, I hate massages. They are so not at all relaxing. Curiously I am better with male masseurs than with women, which probably says a lot about me. The massage I wrote about in this column was a present from my ex on my birthday and even though it was a real treat I was approaching it as a necessary evil and something I had to get through before being able to go to my other birthday treat – a talk at The Sloth Appreciation Society. That probably says even more about me.*

## My Birthday Massage Has a Happy Ending.

My girlfriend has booked me a massage for my birthday to "help me relax". The trouble is, the thought of a massage is stressing me out. I really don't need to be kneaded.

I know that going to a spa is meant to be a relaxing experience, but for me it could be more accurately described as an angst-ridden cringe-fest. All that touching, and the pressure to relax. I also dread getting a female masseuse. What if they discover I'm a lesbian? They might think I came along for an expensive grope.

I'm so tense right now I could be an extra in Silent Witness. "Just relax," says the female masseuse. It's easy for her to say. She's not the one with a sheet of thin tracing paper covering what's left of her modesty. I'm not a size 8, so I think most of my modesty has already bolted.

In an effort to relax me she puts on, Now That's What I Call Spa Music 37. God not the whale music! If whales were subjected to Olly Murs every they got a massage Greenpeace would be launching Rainbow Warrior, but for some reason it's considered an acceptable level of cruelty for humans.

"How are you feeling?" That's women for you. It's not enough that she's seen me naked. Now she wants to know how I'm feeling. I'm no good at talking about feelings at the best of times. But talking about feelings to the crotch of a woman I don't know, with my face crammed into a white padded bum-hole, is a fresh hell. "Fine" I say limply.

"So, have you got any plans for tonight?". Thankfully she's decided to engage me in some chat, but before I can edit myself I tell the truth. "I'm going to a lecture on sloths." She stops touching me. The room goes silent, even the whales have stopped groaning. "That's er int-eresting," she says. Oh God now she thinks I'm a total geek. A geek in a paper g-string.

I can't believe my girlfriend finds THIS relaxing. To recap: I'm in paper pants, being touched by a woman I don't know, to the soundtrack of mating whales, making small talk about sloths.

The absurdity of the situation hits me and I get the giggles. The sort of uncontrollable giggles you only get in serious situations when you know you really shouldn't laugh. Before I can apologise she's seen the funny side and begins to laugh too. My tension instantly dissolves, and for the first time I relax and enjoy myself. At last I've had a massage with a happy ending.

*Getting up close and personal with a bloke and being flirted with is funny sometimes and this was one of those times. It was clearly part of this bloke's patter and he thought I looked sexy so I warmed to him eventually.*

## Seeing Eye-To-Eye With My Optician.

I knew the second the optician winked at me, I should have gone to Specsavers.

He showed me to a seat before he finished flirting with the cute woman he was already serving. Not only was she visually impaired, sadly she also had a screw loose – literally and figuratively. She was actually humouring this man and smiled politely when he offered to give her a "free screw".

This cringeworthy exchange over, he turned his sights on me "Why is your boyfriend not here to help you choose glasses?" Hmm, let me think … because he's playing fantasy football with Santa Claus, the Easter Bunny and the Tooth Fairy. (They don't exist either!)

I came for an eye test, not an inquisition, so instead of getting into it, I mumble something about him being "busy".

Don't get me wrong, I like to flirt with men as much as the next lesbian but this guy with his huge ego and equally huge rims had zero specs appeaI. I wanted to warn him that I was impervious to his charm, that he could not penetrate my sleeze-proof vest, and that any moment I was going to whip out my lesbian card and caution him against inappropriate flirting. Instead, I just tried to avoid eye contact.

We adjourn downstairs to a darkened room and I am suddenly alone with him and his instruments. That's when the nasal noise begins. He starts making that loud noise – those big exhalations of air – that only men make. He sounds like a walrus yawning. The room is so small I'm worried I'm going to be inhaled.

I'd forgotten that opticians are really in your face. The last time a bloke got this close to me Oasis had a #1 single. He instructs me to look straight ahead but all I can focus on is his nostril hair. It's out of control. He looks me in the eyes and asks, "better with or without?" Definitely better without – get it trimmed.

Back upstairs and his verdict is in: I need reading glasses. He picks out some glasses for me to try, and is even able to make my having a wide face sound like a positive. "Those look geeky sexy," he says approvingly as I try on some frames, and quickly qualifies, "...with the emphasis on sexy". I'm starting to like this guy.

He was right, I don't usually suit glasses but these ones weren't bad. Maybe he wasn't that awful after all. He wasn't a sleeze; he was actually quite charming.

Clearly I had been a little short-sighted.

*I'm almost too embarrassed to write anything more for this one. I just thought it was amusing that the fact our cats had different surnames sparked a whole awkward coming out hell right by the catnip cigars.*

## A Soapy Revelation at the Vet.

Last night I was in the bath and reached out to pet my cat with bubble bath on my hand. She proceeded to run off and start licking herself immediately (she's not a fan of Jo Malone) and now I'm concerned that the bubble bath might have permeated her and she's going to become a foaming feline. Obviously I've dashed her to the vets, and now we're waiting in reception.

"Name?" I hate this bit. Whose name does she want, mine or the cat's? "Minnie" I respond confidently, feeling faintly ridiculous. "Surname?" Oh God I don't know. What is my cat's surname? "Westwood." The nurse looks at me with suspicion. It sounds a bit trampy not to know the surname of the cat you lived with for five years. She offers me a few alternatives from the computer. "Yes, that's my girlfriend. The name. Not the cat. Obviously." The joke is not well received.

God, I've just come out at the vets, right there between the catnip cigars and the Science Diet pouches. Oh well, in for a penny in for a pound. The receptionist continues, "And what appears to be the problem with Minnie?" I'm quite stressed at this point, imagining my cat's insides expanding with soapy suds, "Well, we were in the bath." A posh woman with a Tibetan terrier puppy stuffed into a tote looks up. I hurriedly qualify. "My girlfriend and I, not the cat." The receptionist is poised to write something but doesn't. I know it's probably not good etiquette to reveal the details of your daily ablutions to a bunch of strangers in the vet's reception, but in this case it's vital context.

I tell her there was bubble bath in the bath. It was Moroccan Rose bubble bath. She does not take note of this. I sense she's still waiting patiently for the answer to her original question. I get to the bit where I touched the cat with bubble bath, and my theory that there was transference of bubble bath so now I'm worried that the cat has ingested some Moroccan Rose bubbles by proxy.

The receptionist is looking down at her keyboard and typing. I can't see her expression but I can sense that she's stifling a laugh. She summarises. "Minnie exposed to bubble bath." Once it was out there I realised how far fetched it sounded. My little lesbian bathing revelation has been trumped by the fact that a grown adult could think a few bubbles would poison a cat. Clearly when you ask ridiculous questions, sexuality takes a back seat to stupidity.

*This was one of my first columns for DIVA magazine where I was exploring some of the awkward situations I encountered. Changing rooms are terrible. Not because I actually look at the women changing but because I don't, because I'm terrified that they might think I fancy them. This time I had my nephew with me and it changed the dynamics and caught me off guard.*

## Out Of My Depth: Awkward Times in the Swimming Pool Changing Room.

This week I ventured deep into the hetero heart of Surrey to take my three-year-old nephew swimming. I love swimming but since coming out I have developed an irrational fear of women's changing rooms. I worry that a badly timed glance means someone might think I fancy them. I'm not ogling but everywhere I turn I see women brazenly drying their bits, flossing their fannys with a hair towel. It's a flesh-fest. As a precaution my rule is no chat and no eye contact; just in and out.

However, now that I have my nephew in tow all bets are off. He is a yummy mummy magnet. His squeals of "Look at my fishy" are starting to draw a crowd. I'm naked and a wall of women is converging on me. I'm out of my depth.

"Ah he's so cute," they coo. Within moments, four naked ladies have me surrounded. I'm in a boob cube. It continues to amaze me how straight women can stand, naked and chatting, hands on hips, as if in a Post Office queue. I try to remain calm, but casual chit-chat's not easy with eight new nipples in the picture.

Don't look at their boobs. Whatever you do, DO NOT look at their boobs!

Dear God, I don't want to, but now that the thought has entered my mind I feel compelled to look. My eyes flick down from their face and up again.

Phew, no one noticed. Got away with it.

I'm like an undercover agent. They think I'm one of them. I should be taking advantage, straight men would give a kidney for this kind of access, but instead I'm awkward and uncomfortable.

Just then my nephew pipes up again, "Why do you both have writing on your back?" What? Oh NO! I realise what he is talking about and before you can say tramp-stamp, I am comparing tattoos with a buff naked lady. She has one foot up on the bench in front of me and is pointing her bum in my face while providing commentary on her tribal markings. I wish that the walls would breach and a torrent of pool water would wash us away.

When the show and tell finally comes to an end I drop my nephew at his swimming class and hit the pool. At last I can enjoy a little breaststroke.

*I think this is the column that a DIVA reader didn't believe was true. I can absolutely assure you it was. My cheeks have only just started to cool down.*

## Out, Very Loud and Not So Proud in Currys.

I do think it's important to be loud and proud, but it's possible I might have just taken that sentiment too literally. I've just broadcast the fact I'm a lesbian to half of Currys Wembley. I wouldn't mind, but I only went in there to test speakers.

I blame the store assistant. He was the one who instructed me to try the sound of my chosen speakers for size. I plugged my phone in, scrolled down to a random playlist, and hit play. He whacked up the volume and gave me a look as if to say "Just wait you're going to be blown away." There was a momentary pause, then a woman's very deep voice came lustily through the speakers saying, "Sapphic Seductions, a collection of erotic short stories…" I'm blown away.

At first I just stare at the dude from Currys and he stares back. I've no idea that this racy little oeuvre is coming from my phone; I thought it must be a mistake. I'm thinking, "Any minute now Rihanna will kick in". But instead it continued, "I could feel the soft silk of my blouse tighten against my chest as I slowly arched my back in…" I glance down and notice my phone is now helpfully displaying an image of a naked woman and the title Sapphic Seductions. Oh hell. I'm wishing I'd gone for the cheaper, less audible speakers, or (better still) headphones.

I know exactly how this happened. A few years ago I was stuck in a Chicago airport lounge with a lot of stuffy businessmen. A heady mix of boredom and Bloody Marys prompted me to search iTunes for lesbian content and I downloaded this audiobook. It was a bit of fun at the time and I've never listened to it since. In fact I had forgotten about its existence. This audiobook had been languishing in my iPhone for the last six years like some lesbian curse, just waiting for an opportunity to be heard again publically. Why now audiobook? Why Currys Wembley?

Coming out as a lesbian is one thing, but coming out as a lesbian fan of erotic audiobooks in a high street electrical store is unconscionable. I would rather it had played some of my guilty pleasure music: Steps, Celine Dion, or even Chris de Burgh. I frantically fumble with my phone in an attempt to silence my Sapphic Seductions, but I'm panicked and fat fingering. I can't make it stop. The couple in the aisle opposite, who have been loudly arguing over extending a television warranty stop what they're doing and listen. Everyone from Home Cinema to Audio falls silent. All that can be heard is the sound of a breathy-voiced narrator and her tale of lesbian office 'romance'. Oh God, where the hell's Rihanna when you need her.

*I've also tried to poke fun at my own assumptions about some straight people and blokes in particular, which is important. I went into mattress shopping believing that it would be awkward and so I made it awkward. Unnecessarily because the guy we bought the bed off was a really nice bloke.*

## The Salesman Of My Dreams: Going Mattress Shopping With My Girlfriend.

I have just heard five words that chilled me to my core. My comfortable foam core. "We need a new mattress." No. No. No. I'll just put my fingers in my ears, like a kid on a car journey, and sing "la la la la", until this discussion goes away. I don't care that our mattress is basically a sinkhole the size of Wales covered with a fitted sheet, or that it recently swallowed both cats whole. I hate mattress shopping.

The reason I hate mattress shopping is this: I can't help feeling that when my girlfriend and I are trying out a mattress in store we're making a sizeable deposit in the salesman's wank bank. I'm not, as my grandmother would have said, "putting tickets on myself." The act of buying a mattress should a pedestrian affair, like buying a coffee table or washing machine, but as a lesbian the experience seems more sexualised.

Over the years we've developed a mattress store modus operandi which allows us to avoid interacting with salesmen. The second the automatic door opens we separate and conduct individual recces, like two people who've never met before wandering around a mattress store. No lesbians here. No siree! After approximately five minutes we'll converge on the daddy of all mattresses, whereupon we poke at it tentatively a couple of times, and give it 'the knuckle push'. Then, no questions asked, we throw money at it and leave.

"Do you both like a hard one?" Oh God it's started. I wheel around to find an eager salesman smiling at us. I shoot my girlfriend a look that says in no uncertain terms, "We are not getting on this bed. No. Way". He senses my reticence and gives the mattress a reassuring little pat. "Jump aboard. You won't know what it's like till you've tried it." Urgh. How predictable. I imagine he's the sort of bloke who would end a tour of his house by opening the door to his bedroom and saying "This is where the magic happens."

My girlfriend disobeys my silent eye command and climbs up onto the mattress. Then she lies rigidly at the edge of one end, like an extra on Silent Witness, waiting for me to join her. "And you," he chirps, "I need to see how you roll together." Oh I bet you do mate. Reluctantly I climb on and move to the edge of the other side. He then occupies the yawning chasm between us, and starts pushing down hard on the bed, as if he's giving it CPR, causing us to bounce up and down. He claims to be demonstrating 'give' – a likely story.

But the more he talks about the features, the more I fall for his patter. I realise he's not at all interested in us, or phased by the fact he's demonstrating to a lesbian couple, he just loves mattresses – loves them. His smile isn't sleazy. It's the joyful expression of someone who totally and utterly believes in the power of a nice firm pocket spring to bring restorative sleep, and order to a chaotic world. I think I might have just found the salesman of my Dreams.

*This happened a long time before I started writing The Rubbish Lesbian but as London Pride rolled around a few years ago I remembered it, and dredged it up again from the depths of my memory where I'd let it languish lest I become embarrassed all over again.*

## Pride Dashed: When a Wedding Clashes With a Gay Celebration.

The downside of July is that wedding season clashes with Pride. Every year I'd look forward to getting down with some lovely lesbians in Soho, only to end up in Harrogate, on a hen night, drinking Sambuca through a kazoo with 14 straight girls I'd never met before.

When my best friend got married a few years back he asked me to be an usher. It would mean missing Pride, but there was some consolation in being able to rock a power suit to the wedding. As a lesbian I've always liked the idea of a three-piece suit. It's very Madonna circa 1989, only minus the monocle. Unfortunately, when I tried the suit on I found it was also minus the Madonna bit too. It was less, Express Yourself, and more, Go Compare. Clearly Madge didn't rent hers from Moss Bros.

I decided to try and improve the situation by getting my waistcoat made sexier. The trouble is I had no idea how to describe what I wanted to the tailor. I'm a lesbian. I didn't inherit my mother's alteration vocabulary. So when I picked up my waistcoat it wasn't what I was expecting. It had been butchered. The back and sides had been cut away and what remained was basically a bib. It has been altered, but unfortunately beyond all recognition.

The problem with my newly designed waistcoat was that the lack of back precluded me from wearing a bra, conical or otherwise. My invite wasn't for 'plus two', so I was forced to borrow some tit tape from one of the bridesmaids to avoid popping out during the ceremony. Tit tape is basically just sticky back plastic for tits. I was aiming for Madonna, but somehow my outfit was veering off in the direction of Blue Peter. At least I could say, "Here's some I taped earlier."

As if things weren't bad enough, the groom's mother insisted on helping me apply the tape, to my bare breasts. She whisked me into a downstairs toilet. Then she jacked up my tits and stood beneath them like a mechanic holding a light under a car engine working out how to fix it. My tits were being mum-handled. I was dying of embarrassment, but she looked perfectly at home. She was wearing reading glasses and concentrating on my right breast as if it was the Telegraph crossword; she'd got 'one down', but she was struggling to get 'two down'.

But as she picked up my left breast a draft blew through the downstairs loo and to my horror I felt my nipples harden involuntarily. I wanted the ground to open up and swallow me. Instead the unlocked door opened to reveal her husband standing in the doorway. Maybe it was shock, but he wasn't in any hurry to leave. He just stood and stared at his wife, who had tape in her mouth and one of my breasts in her hand. It could have been worse I suppose. It could have been the other way around.

Happily, as wedding season approaches again, there will be no such lapse in Pride this year, because for once I'll be in Soho where I belong.

*A broken table, a fractured toe and another laugh at my own expense here.*

## Dropping a Table, and the L-Bomb.

When blokes find out I'm a lesbian they usually stop flirting with me immediately and move on, so quickly in fact that I need a brace for my conversational whiplash. I'll think we're getting on really well, and they seem really interested to get to know me, but once I've dropped the L-bomb it all goes a bit monosyllabic. If they're no longer interested in me 'in that way', and that they know they're going to crash and burn, they simply pull the rip chord mid-conversation. Sometimes you can see them scrambling to shut off the flirt valve to prevent valuable chat up lines being wasted on me. It must be an evolutionary response – perhaps something to do with ensuring the survival of the human race.

So when a young delivery bloke, who was helping me carry a new table into my flat, became a little overly friendly, I just thought, "Oh here we go again." It was unfortunate really, because a few moments before I'd been staring down his arse crack as he bent down to re-adjust his grip. It was strangely hypnotic, like gazing into the Abyss, but I'd be terrified to share a bed with that. How could you sleep knowing that at any given moment he could turn over and you could be plunged head first into that deep, dark crevasse? It'd be like a scene in Touching the Void, except avoiding touching, of course, of any description.

The problem was that the delivery guy and I had become very close very quickly, but then humping a table up a very steep ramp together will establish that kind of premature intimacy. So it was no surprise to me that once we'd heaved the flat pack across the threshold of my flat he casually dropped the question

"Have you got a bloke?" There it was. I knew it. He was asking if I have a boyfriend – that old chestnut.

It's a tricky question to navigate. I could have answered truthfully and said, "no", but that might have suggested that I'm single, perhaps straight, and therefore fair game. At the same time I didn't really want to out myself to the delivery guy, amiable as he seemed. It felt like way too much intimacy too soon, even given that I was familiar with what brand of underpants he wore. But I've learned from experience that it's best to nip these things in the bud and avoid any ambiguity, so I jumped in with both feet and said it, "No. Actually I'm a lesbian."

The genial chit-chat came to a grinding halt, and he looked genuinely stunned for a moment. Poor guy, I thought. He probably had no idea, and now he's a bit embarrassed that he was flirting with me, and he's working out how to get out of here quick because I'm no longer a good prospect. But somewhat surprisingly he smiled, then gestured over to the assembly instructions. "I only asked because it's a two-man job, love. You're going to need a hand putting it together."

*What can I say? It's possible to go on holiday but it's not always possible to escape from awkward situations. I went to the same resort a year after I wrote this column and Liz came around to introduce herself. Fortunately she didn't remember me, or maybe she just didn't recognise me with my clothes on?*

## Bikini-Clad Awkwardness Anyone? Outed by the Holiday Rep.

Like many lesbian couples my girlfriend and I find booking the right holiday tricky. Many resorts are so geared towards straight couples that we feel conspicuous; like a couple of penguins in dark glasses trying to get into the White House Christmas party. Forget Japanese Kanji symbols, we may as well have 'different' tattooed on our lower backs.

Instructed last year to, "book a romantic holiday" I panicked and delegated the task to my mum's septuagenarian travel agent. Despite being called Les he was clueless about the needs of the Sapphic traveller. He booked us a twin room in an uptight hotel, where we felt it necessary to keep our poolside PDA to a minimum. I spent my days seething behind a Patricia Cornwell at the sight of my fellow straight guests getting it on in public with gay abandon.

This year I didn't take any chances. I booked a spot where I knew we'd be alone. As soon as we arrive I begin extolling the virtues of our remote location. "This is what it's all about. Just us. Alone. This is what I call a holiday." I'm just about to nuzzle up to my girlfriend on the sunbed, when a woman appears from out of the bushes bellowing, "HALLO!". Instinctively we leap up as if we've been scalded, and separate.

Minutes later, we're standing in our shiny underwear (bikinis) being interrogated by a very perky rep named Liz. "So, who got lucky?" she asks enthusiastically. What? That's a bit forward. She's clearly mistaken my red-faced embarrassment with a post-coital flush. Then she clarifies. "Who got the big bedroom?" Oh dear. Liz isn't that forward after all. She's actually a few steps behind.

"We're sharing that room." I accompany the statement with a hard stare for emphasis. My revelation does a number on Liz's well-honed rep patter and she gets a sudden dose of verbal diarrhoea, "YES. Of course! Great! Well why not? Share I mean. Why not share? Why wouldn't you? GREAT. Lovely. Lovely room. Perfect for sharing. Great. Lovely."

I can see that being the meat in our bikini-clad-lesbian sandwich is making Liz visibly uncomfortable. She can no longer hold eye contact. When she catches my eye she immediately looks down at my chest, then panics at the sight of my boobs, looks up, and the whole cycle begins again. The trouble is it's contagious. When she looks down at my chest I return her look, and then look down at hers. My girlfriend is following our little back and forth like a spectator at a tit tennis match.

"Well. I'd better get off now." Liz directs this statement to my breasts who decline to comment, and then disappears back through the bushes leaving us to free to enjoy our holiday. No Les, no Liz, just us lesbians.

*We've all been caught looking, or in my case not really looking, at someone's boobs. We've all been there, right ladies? Come on, back me up here.*

## The Sun's Popped Out, and I'm Busted.

The sunshine is out and so too are the boobs. Yesterday, no breasts, but today summer's arrived, and they've popped out overnight, like the hostas my mum gave me.

Everywhere I look there's cleavage-heaving. On the one hand it's quite a joyous sight, but I really don't want to be caught looking because I'd feel like a tit, so it's a double edged sword; a case of what God giveth with one handful he takes with the other. Quiet appreciation of another woman's cleavage at a glance is fine, but staring down into it the way blokes do is not.

I used to work with a guy who'd spend entire meetings ignoring my face, and speaking exclusively to my sweater stretchers – he never once saw my lips move. I was like a breast ventriloquist. I should have really wowed him by drinking a glass of water while they sang him a song.

Believe me fellas, I understand that breasticles are very pretty an' all, but come on. Get a grip. In fact don't get a grip – stay the hell away!

Then I had an 'incident'. A woman sat down opposite me at a meeting, and I knew immediately I had a cleavage situation. She has a low cut top on, and with every breath she took it appeared that the fun bags she'd packed were getting ready to vacate her bra. I began mentally preparing to jump up and throw my cardy over her to protect her modesty.

To make matters worse my eye caught a flash of something right in the middle of her cleavage. A little bit of metal had poked through the lace of her bra, and every time she moved it glinted. It was mesmerising, like a lure, and if I wasn't careful I was going to get caught – staring.

Look up. Look up. Carol Anne, listen to me! Do not go into the light!

Dear God, if she caught me she'd think I was staring at her baps. I tried mainlining custard creams to take my mind off her broken bra, but it was no good. Even the taste of moist custard powder and vegetable fat wasn't enough to distract me.

Surely that bit of metal would hurt? It needed to be fixed, forced back inside the underwire. My eyes flicked down again for only a second to assess the damage, but this time when I looked up again she was smiling at me. It was my worst nightmare. She'd caught me looking. Busted.

*I felt like I was starring in a lesbian remake of a Billy Ocean video recently when I bumped into someone I almost had a fling with (why is there no word for this type of relationship?). Except she didn't so much get into my car as onto the bonnet of my sister's Corsa. Let's just say our reunion didn't play out the way I had always imagined it would. This one is for my friend Robyn who has promised to retell this story at my wake should I go first.*

## This is Not My Corsa: Bumping Into An Old Flame.

I've borrowed my little sister's car for the weekend and I'm just about to return it. She's very generous; her motto is 'Mi Corsa e su Corsa.' On my way to drop it off an old flame steps straight out of my past and almost onto the bonnet. The lady in question is older than me, and a sophisticate. When we dated she had two of the things I most wanted in the world: a dog and a Porsche 911. For me at the time they were the ultimate symbols of lesbian chic. She'd swing by to pick me up for a date, dog barking a welcome, the Porsche growling seductively. That was one sexy beast – the Porsche, not the dog. Did I mention that she drove a lust-inspiring Porsche?

This woman and I didn't have a relationship as such, but we did go on a lot of 'sort of dates'; she'd pick me up for nice walks, we'd lie around in the park on blankets chatting, but nothing ever happened. I think she was unsure about whether I was actually a lesbian and to be honest so was I. So we were in this kind of no man's land between friendship and more. In the end it fizzled out. She never called me. Things. Just. Stopped.

I've often thought about that Porsche, I mean that period in my life and this particular woman, since coming out. Every time

I'd imagine bumping into her again I too now had a dog and a sports car. She'd see me and with a sad smile of regret think of me as the one that got away. My hair is long in this particular daydream. I'm wearing a sassy little summer dress, and my hound is sitting adorably in the passenger seat as I pull up to her bumper, tunes blaring, in my very own Porsche.

So having her almost slide up onto the bonnet of my sister's Corsa was not ideal. Nor was my outfit, a tracksuit, and the fact that I was wearing no make-up. I screeched to a halt and for a moment she looked in angrily. Then she registered who it was and there was a flick of recognition. A second later I saw she'd clocked the two baby seats in the back. NO!! Inside I was screaming NO! This is not me. This is not my Corsa! But it was useless. Her smile of vindication said "Yep, straight after all".

PART NINE

# OTHER LESBIANS

## My Faulty Gaydar, Adventures in Lesbian Bars and Mastering the Lesbian Nod.

*I grew up in a small town where there were no out gay people. In 1988, we were still getting over the arrival of the town's first Chinese restaurant. You were considered 'alternative' if you didn't order chips with your chow mein. Needless to say I didn't have any lesbian role models growing up.*

*Dealing with other lesbians when I first came out was a problem. I'd steel myself to go to lesbian bars, but I always left feeling inadequate, or intimidated. Some lesbians I met didn't want to accept me, maybe because I had long hair, or because I'd had boyfriends in the past.*

*The columns in this section reveal a desire to fit in and to be accepted, but also a realisation that I had to be myself.*

*I have terrible gaydar. People assume that because you're gay you'll be able to spot another gay a mile off. I was that one person who was surprised when Ellen came out.*

## I Need a Gaydar Upgrade.

It's 3pm on Monday and I'm at home in the middle of the afternoon waiting for the Gaydar repairman. This is the second time in as many days that the signal's gone on the blink. Every time I walk past the microwave it picks up Radio 4.

Yesterday I couldn't tell whether the woman who served me in Pret A Manger was a lesbian or just very attentive. She held my gaze, and the other end of my baguette, a little longer than was comfortable. It felt like a lesbian handoff but I couldn't be sure. I couldn't read the signal.

I've never been very good at picking up gay vibes. A few weeks ago I was convinced that a client was a lesbian, but it turned out she wasn't. She was from Prague.

Straight friends always nudge me and ask "is she or isn't she?" when they see a 'questionable' girl, as if I have innate powers of detection. (I don't.) My Gaydar is temperamental and long range; I can't tell if someone is a lesbian until she's on top of me.

I blame my equipment. It's first generation, soon-to-be-obsolete technology. I don't have the Hipster Filter so trendy areas like Shoreditch are a no-go, because every girl I pass sets it off. Likewise, it doesn't have Predictive Bieber, which means I'm always in danger of cosying up to teenage boys at bus stops.

Don't even get me started on rural coverage. The countryside is one big black spot. The last time I left London I had to climb a hill to get a signal. It came on for two minutes, caught a woman in a North Face fleece, and went off so loudly it scared the sheep.

I also have the reverse problem. Too many stealth lesbians elude my detection by looking straight. They are entirely invisible. Only people with a sixth sense can see and talk to them, and I can't see lesbians.

At 5pm the repairman eventually shows up. He turns my Gaydar off and on repeatedly, sucks his teeth and gives his diagnosis: "It's bust." The good news is that I am due an upgrade. I'm getting the iGaydar 5 with Nasa technology. It has speech recognition software and gesture identification, so there will be no more women slipping under my Gaydar.

*This date happened after I replied to an advert on Guardian Soulmates, so I guess you could say that I brought this on myself. We made out over bangers and mash watching Dirty Dancing, but it wasn't meant to be.*

## Sadly, Not Gay Enough for One Girl.

It was the summer of 69. Okay, it was the summer of 2003. While the rest of Britain sweltered in a heat wave, I was getting hot under the collar about my first official date with a woman. She was a real live, beautiful, in the flesh, actual lesbian person. Beyoncé was playing out of every car window, and I was 'crazy in love'.

I was newly out and I'd already found my perfect woman: she liked guinea pigs AND Grease 2. I asked her out for a drink and she accepted. I felt like The Lezmeister.

A few drinks in and things seemed to be going well. It was SO on. I had started mentally moving her into my flat when she leant towards me, and in her sexiest voice whispered, "You're not gay enough."

To recap: I was out on a date – with another woman. I felt like a lesbian – I felt like that lovely lesbian until she dropped this bomb on me. How could she think I wasn't lez enough?

This was a major blow to my fledgling lesbian career. I can only think that 'looking straight' and having straight friends suggested that I wasn't fully committed. Apparently it was grounds for instant dismissal of my sexuality.

I felt a sort of in between-ness; I wasn't straight but I looked it, and even though I was a lesbian, I didn't exactly fit that mould either. I found myself in No Man's Land and it wasn't nearly as much fun as it sounded.

I'd expected lesbians all across London to welcome me with open arms. But a year after coming out there were still no quiches being baked in my honour. I wasn't hiding, they just didn't see me. I was caught in their collective blind spot; I had to wear a Hi-Vis vest top.

Last week I came across my erstwhile crush on a social network site, and guess what? She now is married – to a man. I'm afraid it's just one more example of the pot calling the kettle an inferior lesbian.

It's taken me a long time to have the confidence to be my own kind of lesbian, and not feel the need to fit anyone else's preconceived ideas of what that means.

Just don't come around asking me to do any printer-cartridge-replacing, oven-light-not-working-fixing or large-spider-removing though, because I'm definitely not lez enough for that.

*Is it just me, or do women become more interesting the moment you find out they're a lesbian? I think that's fact.*

## The Lesbian Effect: It Makes Women More Interesting.

I'm not sure why it is, but when I find out that someone is a lesbian they become exponentially more interesting. I call it 'The Lesbian Effect'. Women I thought were funny get funnier, clever women become geniuses, and even attractiveness is increased threefold.

It happened recently with someone I met through work. The more I saw her in action, the more I became convinced that she was lesbian, and by definition more interesting. I noticed she had a 'way' about her, like she was packing some serious attitude. We hadn't exchanged much more than conspiratorial looks over soy cappuccinos, but I could tell that I liked her.

I didn't think for one moment she was straight. She couldn't be, she was far too interesting. I pictured her going home to her artsy flat, and her artsy girlfriend, and reciting Balzac in the bath.

So I really wasn't prepared for her to say, "What does your boyfriend think about you working late? Mine hates it."

What? How could she think I was straight? How could she be straight?

I said, "Girlfriend actually", to which she replied, "Oh really. You'd never guess...from the way you are."

What? What 'way' is that? I thought she was the one with the 'way'. Now I'm confused, somehow we've got our ways crossed.

As the conversation goes on, all her 'interesting' begins to fall off. I discover that her 'way' – which moments earlier I'd found charming – is actually just plain gruff and unattractive. I've mistaken a brusque demeanour for a sexy lesbian attitude. Blerg.

I hear the thud of high expectations hitting the floor, or was it was the sound of her falling from grace?

But then The Lesbian Effect begins to work in reverse. I've become more interesting to her. Her stock is falling, but mine is rising. I've gone from common-or-garden straight girl to exciting lesbian. I can sense her desire to add me to her 'collection' of 'alternative' friends. Evidently she doesn't have 'a lesbian' friend. Out lesbians are as rare as hen's teeth apparently, which makes me dinner party gold.

Now, she's floating the idea of us going for drinks to catch up properly. That's clearly code for her to interrogate me in the back room of a pub. Oh god, she wants a trophy lesbian. I need to leave now before she has me stuffed and mounted.

*When I first came out I tried going to a couple of lesbian bars on my own. I always felt like an outsider. When I met my ex-girlfriend we must have tried every lesbian bar in every town we ever went to in search of the perfect lesbian bar experience. With the exception of the one I wrote about in this column in Paris, the best one I have come across is The Cubby Hole in New York. We had many fun times in that bar drinking Amstel Light and playing Bad Romance on their legendary jukebox.*

## Lesbian Bars Are Not My Scene.

"Ah, Paris! City of Love. City of Lights. City of…"

"Lesbian bars?"

My girlfriend is flicking through a guidebook calling out things to do in Paris. Lesbian bars are not really my scene. I'm more of an 'armchair lesbian'; I enjoy The Candy Bar from the comfort of my living room. I stand a far greater chance of being propositioned there, and the beer is cheaper.

My early experiences of lesbian bars were not positive; I never felt I belonged. I'd sneak in, sit at the bar, nurse a beer and then leave without ever making eye contact. I was in and out – and out and in again – within minutes. To make matters worse I was always mistaken for a straight girl. Women gave me a wide berth, like I was a marked down M&S prawn sandwich.

I have flirted with one or two lesbian bars since then, but I've never found one I really liked. My last foray into the lesbian scene was a few years ago in New York. We must have examined every lesbian joint in the Big Apple, and my diagnosis was always bad news. Bars were either 'too empty' or 'too scary', or I felt 'too young' or 'too old'.

I feel like Goldilocks searching for the perfect lesbian bar: I'm Goldilez.

After a few glasses of red wine we decide to sample Gay Paree. I'm excited about dipping my toe into the Parisian Sapphic Scène. I picture chic women drinking red wine and discussing Derrida, subdued lighting, a smoky atmosphere, and the seductive sound of Edith Piaf.

We round the corner and come face to facade with bar number one. First impressions aren't good: there is a woman in a buffalo stance blocking the doorway. The bar itself is pitch black inside. The regulars are so accustomed to the dark that they emerge and stand like pit ponies, while their eyes readjust to the light.

I whisper "Too dark!" to my girlfriend, and we keep walking. I'm hoping that the next bar will be better.

It's not better. The lighting in this bar is a retina-burning bright pink, and Gaga is registering a seven on the Richter scale. I have to mouth, "Too bright AND too loud".

I can tell that my girlfriend is running dangerously low on patience, but luckily bar number three is completely different. It has a refreshingly genial ambience. The women are diverse, relaxed and friendly. Culture Club is playing in the background, but it is still possible to hear the sound of mojitos being mashed. The decor is funky, not pink. It's not too bright, or too loud.

"Ahh this lesbian bar is 'just right'."

*I have no idea when women are flirting with me. I think they're just being friendly. I think it's a heterosexual throwback.*

## Flirting With Disaster: Caught With Ink On My Face.

I have been abandoned. My girlfriend and I are in a lesbian bar and she's gone to the bathroom, leaving me unattended. I'm waiting obediently like a dog tethered outside Tesco, my eyes trained on the bathroom door ready to jump up expectantly at the sight of my mistress returning.

So here I am. Sitting. By myself. In a bar. On my own. Alone. It's fine. It's not fine. I can't believe she's left me alone! Talk about irresponsible! What if people don't realise I'm taken? What if I get pinched? Loyal girlfriends are stolen everyday in situations just like this, lured away with a few scraps of attention. If she doesn't hurry back soon, I'm worried I'll be 'rescued' and re-homed faster than I can say, "Make mine a Corona."

*Just keep your eyes down. Do NOT catch anyone's eye.*

I've caught someone's eye. A girl at the end of the bar is smiling at me and touching her forehead.

*Don't smile. Do not smile. Look away.*

I've smiled back. We're playing smile tennis. It's official. I'm flirting.

She looks me in the eyes and strokes her forehead a few more times. All I can think is – *I've still got it!*

I thought I'd be rusty, but no, this Mexican beer is like WD40 on my flirt valve; it's beginning to loosen and she's continuing to touch her forehead. I've even got a little routine going; I take a sip of beer followed by a nonchalant stretch, and then a perfectly executed head-tilted smile. Either I'm flirting, or I've just invented Corona Yoga.

I'm having so much fun I don't even notice my girlfriend has returned. She taps me on the back and I wheel around to find her staring at me with an expression I can't quite read. Is it anger or bemusement?

"What's that on your face?' she asks.

Oh God. It's guilt. She is actually reading the guilt on my face. It was only innocent flirting. It was her fault for leaving me. She knows I have a short attention span and can't self-soothe.

"How did you manage to transfer your hand-stamp to your forehead?"

Oh no. I think I just discovered the reason that girl was 'flirting' with me. Pssssst. I hear the sound of the air escaping from my inflated ego. I should never be left on my own.

*Remind me to tell you about the time I was introduced to Rachel Weiss at a party in New York. It didn't go well. Or the time I chatted to Chrissie Hyde in the queue to buy fags. I've also discussed the pros and cons of salt and vinegar crisps with Debbie Harry.*

## How to Survive a Celesbian-Packed Party.

I've just realised that the Heather Peace launch party I'm attending is wall-to-wall celebrities. They're everywhere. It's the Celesbian equivalent of the Christmas Island crab migration. I'll have to stand in one spot all night to avoid stepping on one. If my previous form with celebrities is anything to go by, this won't end well. In fact, it's statistically more likely to end in embarrassment.

I've learned not to embrace anyone like a long-lost friend in case they're famous and I don't actually know them at all. I had a Dirty Dancing 'watermelon moment' at Wimbledon, when I greeted Virginia Wade with an enthusiasm rarely seen outside of the arrivals hall at Heathrow. She left, and I spent the next ten minutes repeating back, "Hello Virginia? Hello Virginia?", in a foetal position.

What's the etiquette if I do meet a celebrity? Is it best to pretend not to know their names? I don't want to appear too eager. Will Alice Arnold and Clare Balding believe that I don't know who they are? I know what they had for breakfast thanks to Twitter. I'd better not open with, "I follow you" or they'll become alarmed and picture me riffling through their bins.

I'm trying to look cool, but Heather Peace just smiled in my direction, and I lost control of my poker face. I was going for 'cooly aloof', but now I'm worried she might have read my expression as bored. It's a very fine facial line. Oh God, she probably thinks I'd rather be at home emptying the lint draw of the tumble dryer.

It's hard not to look at the celebrities, but I can't be seen to be stargazing. I'm surreptitiously scanning the room like the old painting with the moving eyes in Scooby Doo. If I spot Jane Hill I will quickly look away. I will not stare at her like a drunk person who's just laid eyes on a Gregg's sausage roll.

I decide to take a 'time out', and I'm just crowbarring myself into the smallest bathroom in the world, when I realise that the only other person in there is Alison Moyet. I stare down at my feet. It's a really tight squeeze. I have to hold my elbows in to avoid them weighing heavy on her bladder. The confined space is amplifying the awkwardness and I'm afraid the situation is about to unravel faster than the gig toilet roll. I have to say something. Think of something cool. Quick.

"I read that people with full bladders make better decisions."

All evidence is clearly pointing to the contrary. What was I thinking? She enters the stall, and I'm forced to chalk it up as another celebrity boob – and not the good kind.

*I noticed that lesbians have a whole secret sign language thing going on. Lesbian strangers can perform full introductions without actually saying a word.*

## The Lesbian Nod: It's Like The Bus-Driver's Wave.

I've just spotted a couple of lesbians in the queue in front of me at the airport. I can't believe it. Lesbians. At the airport. What could they possibly be doing here?

I love lesbian spotting. It's like the frisson of excitement you get from seeing such a rare bird where you least expect too. I feel the need to record my sighting like some sort of enthusiastic twitcher. I'm not superstitious, but if I see a pair of lesbians they have to be saluted.

I get a bit over excited when I spot another lesbian couple. Sometimes you can go months without seeing one. The longer the gap between sightings, the more my anticipation builds. Then boom! When it happens it's like finally turning over a card that matches my own. I'm desperate to be the first to call out "Snap!".

But apparently that kind of reaction is not good form. If you and your partner pass another lesbian couple on the street, you must make eye contact, smile and do a little nod and a chin lift, before continuing gaily on your way. Them's the rules.

So I know that when the couple in front of me spots me I'll have to perform a, lesbian nod. It's a silent acknowledgement, like the little wave that bus drivers do when they pass another bus driver, but far more stealth. It's a silent Sapphic approval between the nodder and noddee that says, "yes, hello, I see you, we both like the ladies."

Unfortunately, I've never quite gotten to grips with the nod; I can't get my nod on. It's the last bit, the chin lift that I can't master. Only an infinitesimal eyebrow raise separates friendly from flirty. I'm so afraid my nod will be mistaken for a come-on that I always fluff it. It looks less like a lesbian nod, and more like I'm suffering from swimmer's ear.

Oh! The lesbians are on the move. They've finished checking in and now they're checking me out. There's only a split-second window for simultaneous acknowledgement. I brace myself and bust out my best nod ever. I've totally nailed it.

But they continue walking. No nod. No smile. Not even a twitch.

I stare back at my girlfriend in disbelief. I quite clearly gave them the nod. They took my nod and didn't return it. To them I'm just another straight girl with swimmer's ear.

*I was aware of the small lesbian world cliché, but it wasn't until recently that I really understood what that meant. Lesbians love to 'network'.*

## The Lesbian Network: Six Inches of Separation.

Lesbians really do love to network. Before everyone was connected via the World Wide Web there was just the lesbian phonebook second edition. Your average lesbian would put Kevin Bacon to shame; most are only five degrees of M&S gusset from each other. We're driven to keep expanding the circle. It's in our DNA. We love a new lesbian, one we haven't met before, it's like the release of a new flavour of Walkers Sensations.

It's not the best start to the lesbian networking event. I arrive 45 minutes late because I had to make a stop at the printers to pick up business cards. I usually forget them but this time I was under strict instructions from a colleague to thrust one at every lesbian I met, and I wasn't going to disappoint.

Trouble is I don't excel at networking. I watch with envy as some people swagger in confidently like they own the place – it's called 'working the room'. After one hour they've left with all the intel they need as if on a military mission of reconnaissance. I slip in undetected and slink around with my back to the wall like an escaping fugitive avoiding a searchlight. I have been known to leave without even exchanging a single pleasantry – let alone business card.

This time I've bought a wing woman but my friend and I are instructed to separate by a woman with a stick-on name badge because after all we're here to make new friends. We promise to look out for each other before going to mingle separately. I'm determined to step up to the canapé plate, bite the sausage-roll-shaped bullet, and grab the bullshit by the horns. I'm going to 'get involved' – after I go back to the bathroom for a quiet sit down.

In truth, once you put aside everything you've ever learned about social skills, and get comfortable with bowling up to a conversation in full flow and bellowing, "Hello! I'm Sarah. Who are you?" things improve. I don't even know why I was so nervous. This networking malarkey is a piece of cake. A few Coronas later and I'm even channelling Deborah Meaden and saying things like, "Here's my card. Call me." Tomorrow morning the phone will be ringing off the hook – guaranteed.

Finally, I thrust my last business card into the hands of the only person not to have received one. She looks at it for a couple of minutes then back at me and says, "Panna Patel?" What? No! Oh crap I've been giving out my straight work colleague's business cards all night rather than my own. You know what this means? I've just achieved something that puzzled ancient geometers for years: I've just straightened the circle.

*Before I came out I'd actively avoid eye contact with any women I thought to be gay in case they spotted that I was also gay. Now I'm happily out it really annoys me when gay women don't acknowledge me.*

## Honest, I'm a Lesbian: A Case of Mistaken Sexual Identity.

It's Friday night and I'm sitting at one of those bland bars inside an equally generic business hotel at Heathrow waiting for a client. It's full of blokes all wearing name-badges, but it's the kind of place where nobody knows your name. So the last thing I was expecting to see here was a lesbian couple smooching at a nearby table.

I can't believe what I'm seeing. They're nibbling each other's necks right there beneath the Lite Bites menu. I imagine all the other customers are staring, but glancing around the room I'm pleasantly surprised to discover a lack of palpable outrage. Nobody is looking at them, in fact everyone appears unconcerned – everyone except me. Now I've noticed the lesbian lovebirds I can't stop staring as they nuzzle noses over a veggie-sharing platter. It's great that they can canoodle over crudité with such impunity. It's a testament to how far we've come.

I've got the urge to let them know I'm 'one of them'. I always acknowledge lesbian strangers with a little wink or a nod. It's the way I roll – it's the sapphic equivalent of Beetle owners giving each other the horn. The blokes in here will be oblivious, because we lesbians communicate in a series of highly evolved signals and subtle cues that are virtually imperceptible to the heterosexual eye.

I give them 'the look' and wait excitedly for my acknowledgement.

But they return my look with disgust. What's going on? My look clearly said, "Hello lesbian friends". They've misread it. I look again and this time they give me a disappointed head shake. Oh no. They've misread my look of camaraderie. They think I'm a disapproving straight woman. They've even started courting sympathetic nods of outrage – at my supposed outrage – from someone at the bar who's labelled himself as John. I'm in a quagmire of silent condemnation and sinking fast.

I must right this wrong, and quickly, before my client arrives. Seizing my opportunity to affirm my lesbian credentials I sidle up to one half of the couple at the bar, hand on hip, and say in a loud stage whisper, "I'm waiting for my misses." There's no flicker of recognition. Louder and deeper voiced I add, "She's always late – my girlfriend." This time she looks right at me. Phew, it worked. She gets it. But her eyes flick over my right shoulder to a person behind me. It's my client. She's been waiting for a suitable time to interrupt and is probably wondering why I said I referred to her as my girlfriend. After a moment's hesitation she introduces herself. "Hello! I'm late." I hold out my hand. "Hello! I'm sorry."

# AFTERWORD

I'm turning over a new lesbian.

Every year like millions of others I make a list of ambitious new year's resolutions that I fully intend to keep: no booze, no lard and no cigarettes. And every year by approximately 9.03am on January 1st they have fallen by the wayside; I'm draining the last dregs of a Bloody Mary and salivating at the sight of some fish fingers under the grill, while simultaneously lighting a cigarette off the gas ring. But this year, while others are attempting to turn over a new leaf, I will be turning over a new lesbian. I've had enough of being rubbish at all things lesbian, so my new year's resolutions are as follows:

1. When the greengrocer remarks, "Where's your 'friend' today?" I shall not look down, banana in hand, and scurry off mumbling something incoherent. No. Instead I shall look him squarely in the eye and say, "Do you mean my lover? She is at home vacuuming summer clothes into storage bags since you ask." Then I will turn my back and sashay out of there. Buoyed by my success I'll probably drop off my car for its annual service, toss the keys at the attending petrol head, and say breezily, "My Mrs will be picking it up."

2. I will no longer dread the holiday check-in for weeks in advance of the trip. And when we arrive at our destination and the inevitable twin room is proffered I won't accept it meekly, slink upstairs, row with my girlfriend, and sleep in the crack for a week. No siree. I will look excitedly around at my fellow holidaymakers and bellow, "Twin Schwin. We require your finest double room please, because we're planning on having so much sex I'll have to bubble wrap my boobs for the trip home."

3. In the gay haven of Soho, where once I would have felt

self-conscious holding my girlfriend's hand, I shall snog with impunity in all weathers – onlookers be damned. From this day forward I will become a positive role model for horny exhibitionist LGBT youth everywhere. My lips shall not rest until everyone has had the positive life-affirming opportunity of seeing me snogging the face off another woman outside an Angus Steakhouse completely undaunted by the muttered comments and odd invitation of a threesome from passers-by.

So that's it then. Resolutions made. I can already tell that 2014 is going to be my year. Look out world here comes the lesbian formerly referred to as rubbish!